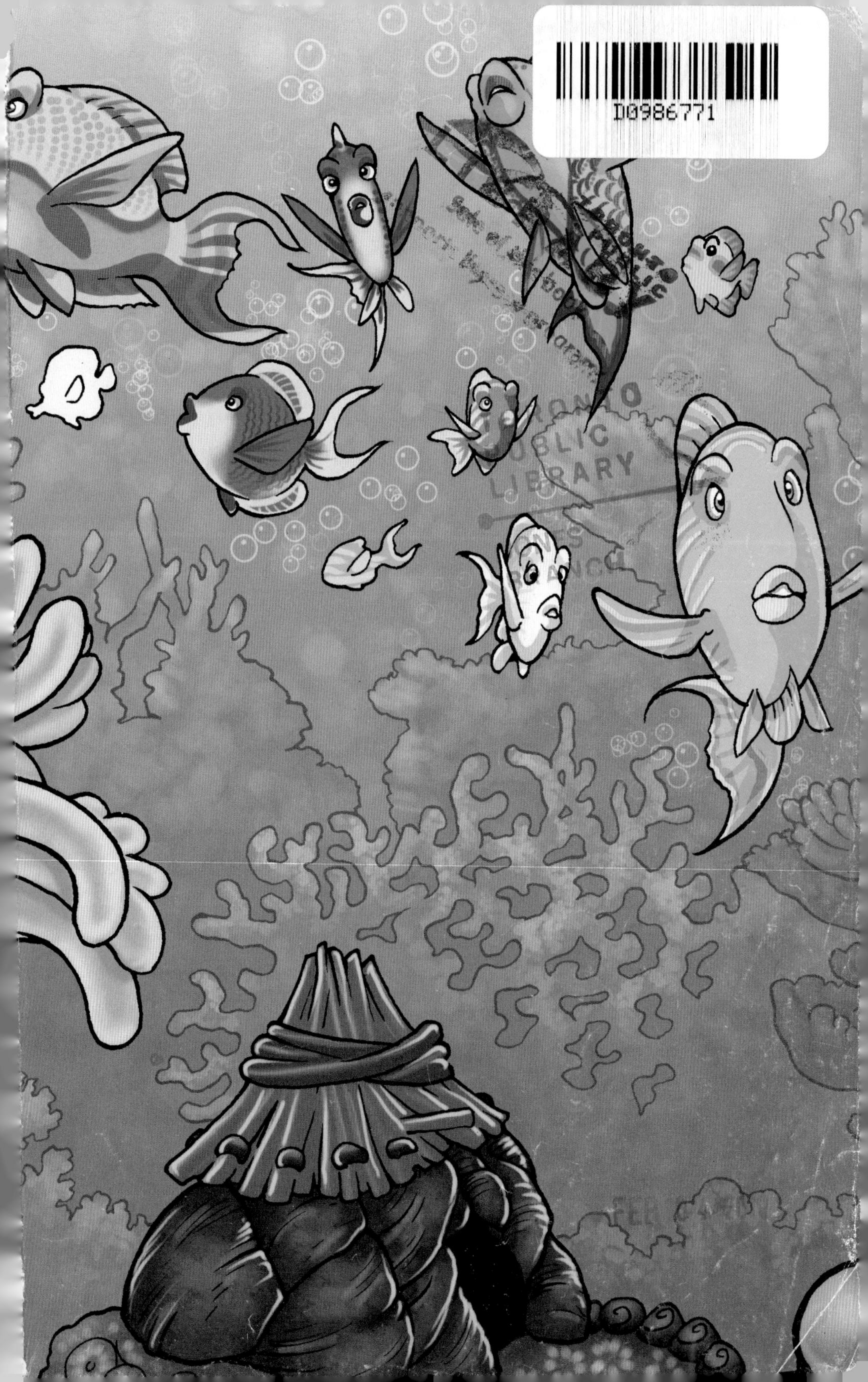

**ROSS RICHIE**
chief executive officer

**ANDREW COSBY**
chief creative officer

**MARK WAID**
editor-in-chief

**ADAM FORTIER**
vice president,
publishing

**CHIP MOSHER**
marketing director

**MATT GAGNON**
managing editor

FIRST EDITION: OCTOBER 2009

10 9 8 7 6 5 4 3 2 1

PRINTED BY WORLD COLOR PRESS, INC.,
ST-ROMUALD, QC., CANADA. 11/26/09

**FINDING NEMO: REEF RESCUE** – published by BOOM Kids!, a division of Boom Entertainment, Inc. All contents © 2009 Disney/Pixar. BOOM Kids! and the BOOM Kids! logo are trademarks of Boom Entertainment, Inc., registered in various countries and categories. All rights reserved.

Office of publication: 6310 San Vicente Blvd Ste 404, Los Angeles, CA 90048.

A catalog record for this book is available from the Library of Congress and on our website at www.boom-studios.com on the Librarian Resource Page.

# FINDING NEMO
## REEF RESCUE

WRITTEN BY
**MARIE CROALL**

ART
**ERICA LEIGH CURREY**

COLORS
**DIGIKORE STUDIOS**
ISSUE 1 & 4

**ERICA LEIGH CURREY**
ISSUE 2

**VERONICA GANDINI**
ISSUE 3

COVER
**ERICA LEIGH CURREY**

LETTERER
**MARSHALL DILLON**

EDITORS
**PAUL MORRISSEY
& AARON SPARROW**

SPECIAL THANKS:
JESSE POST, LAUREN KRESSEL
AND ELENA GARBO

# CHAPTER ONE

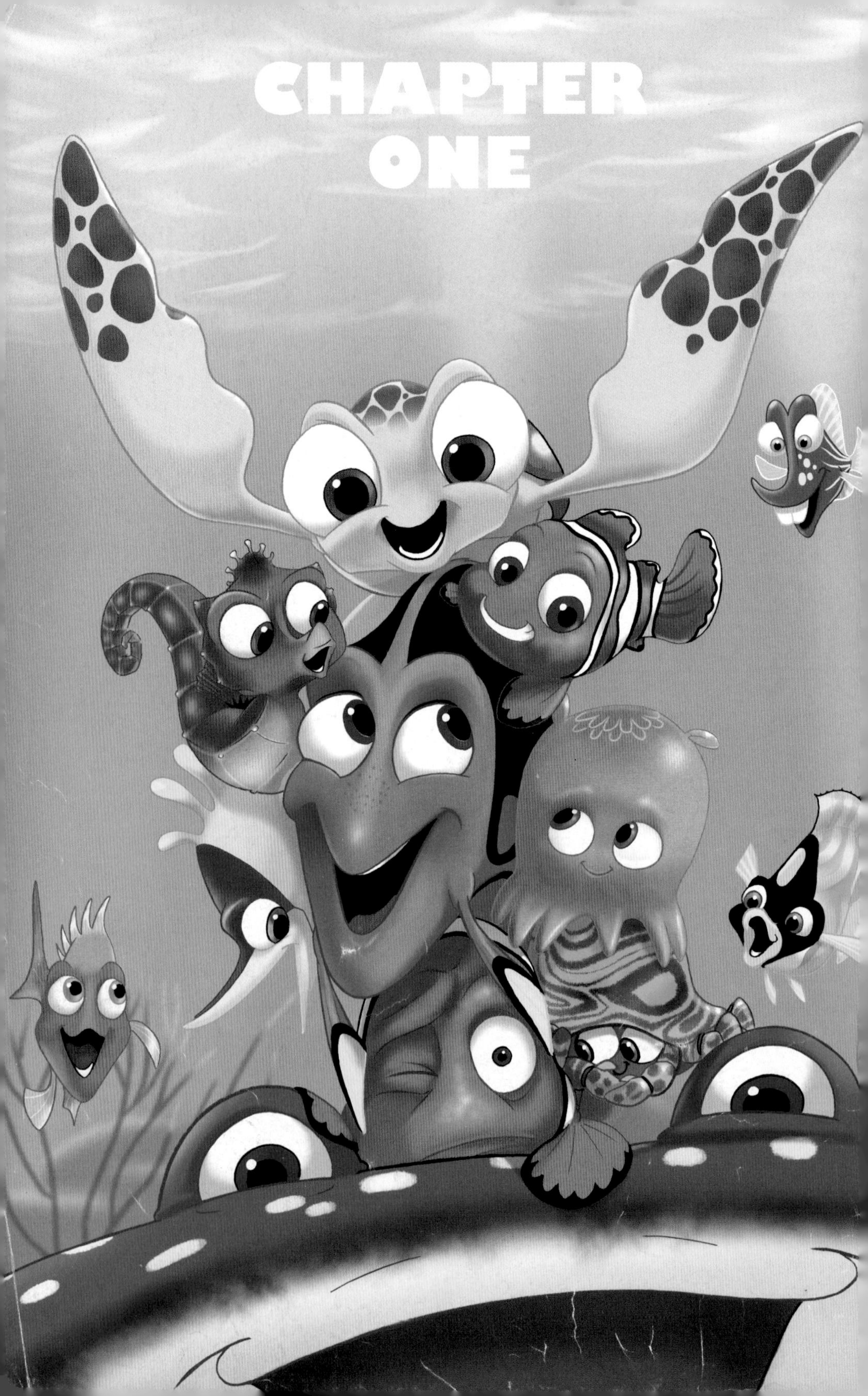

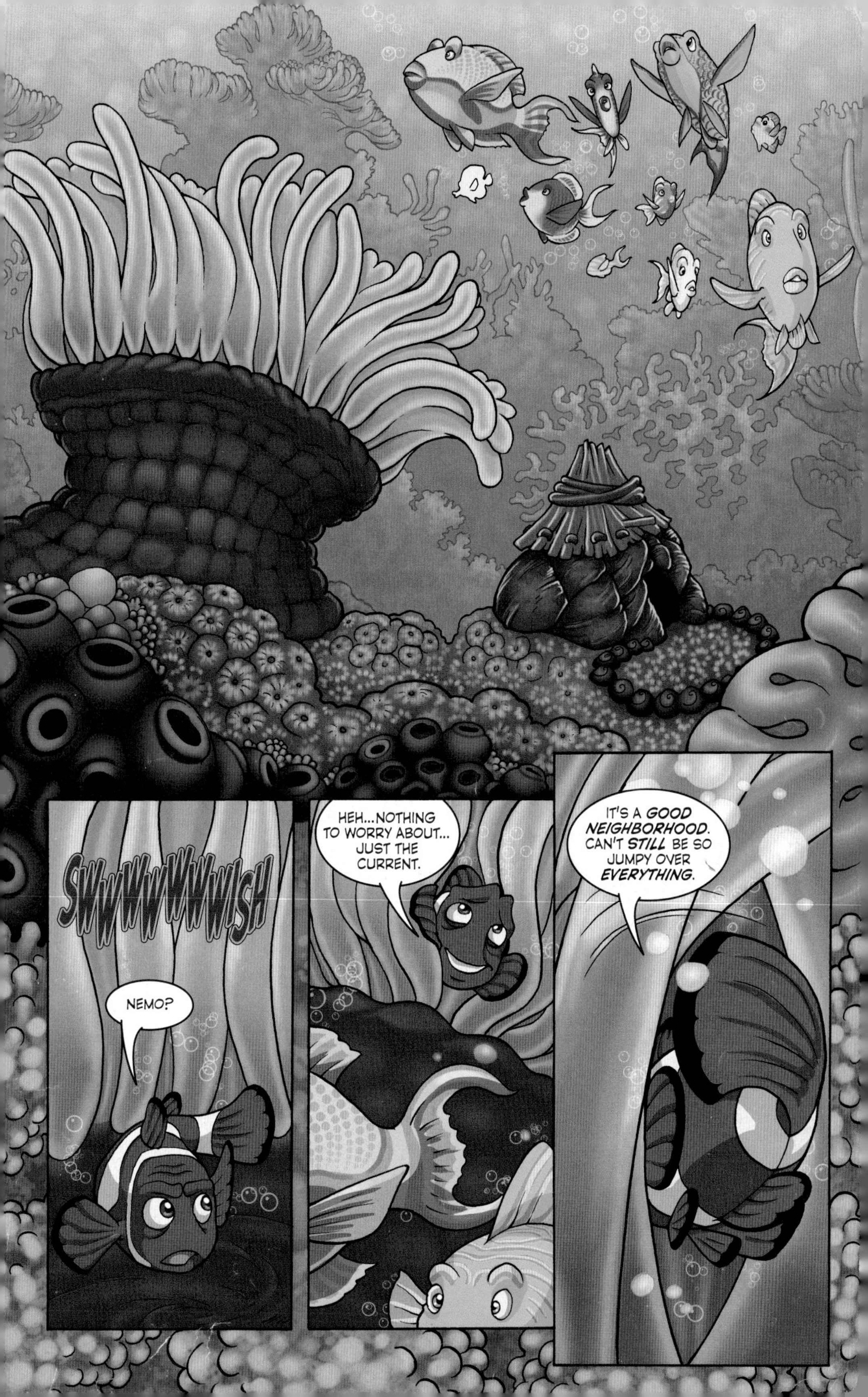
SWWWWWWWISH
NEMO?
HEH...NOTHING TO WORRY ABOUT... JUST THE CURRENT.
IT'S A *GOOD NEIGHBORHOOD*. CAN'T *STILL* BE SO JUMPY OVER *EVERYTHING*.

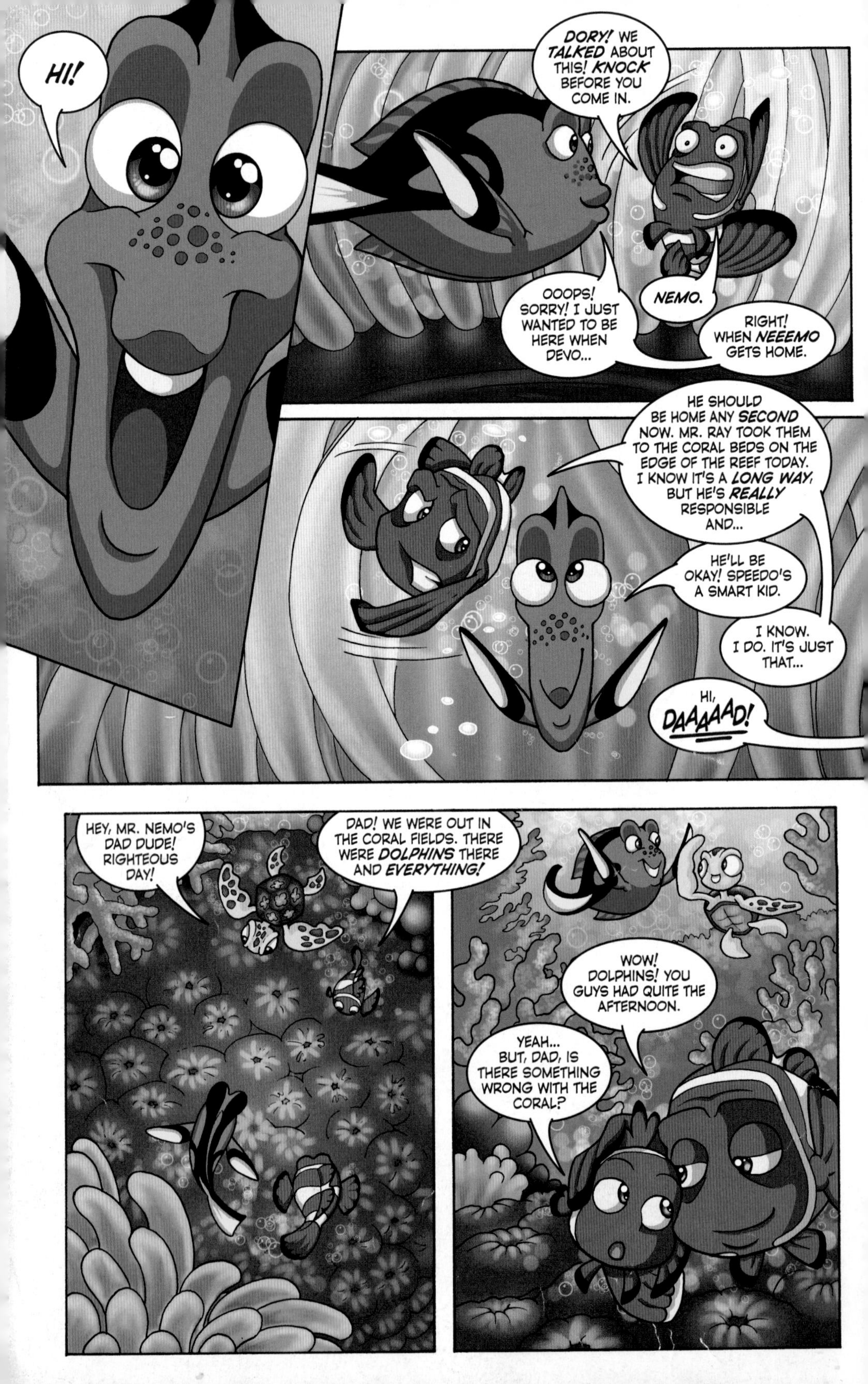
HI!
DORY! WE TALKED ABOUT THIS! KNOCK BEFORE YOU COME IN.
OOOPS! SORRY! I JUST WANTED TO BE HERE WHEN DEVO...
NEMO.
RIGHT! WHEN NEEEMO GETS HOME.
HE SHOULD BE HOME ANY SECOND NOW. MR. RAY TOOK THEM TO THE CORAL BEDS ON THE EDGE OF THE REEF TODAY. I KNOW IT'S A LONG WAY, BUT HE'S REALLY RESPONSIBLE AND...
HE'LL BE OKAY! SPEEDO'S A SMART KID.
I KNOW. I DO. IT'S JUST THAT...
HI, DAAAAAD!
HEY, MR. NEMO'S DAD DUDE! RIGHTEOUS DAY!
DAD! WE WERE OUT IN THE CORAL FIELDS. THERE WERE DOLPHINS THERE AND EVERYTHING!
WOW! DOLPHINS! YOU GUYS HAD QUITE THE AFTERNOON.
YEAH... BUT, DAD, IS THERE SOMETHING WRONG WITH THE CORAL?

THE CORAL? OF *COURSE NOT.* WE WOULD KNOW IF SOMETHING WAS WRONG.

'CAUSE WHEN WE WERE OUT THERE TODAY, MR. RAY SAID IT LOOKED *SICK.*

COME ON, NEMO. WE CAN TALK ABOUT THIS AT HOME.

CATCH YA' LATER, FISH DUDES! GOOD LUCK, NEMO!

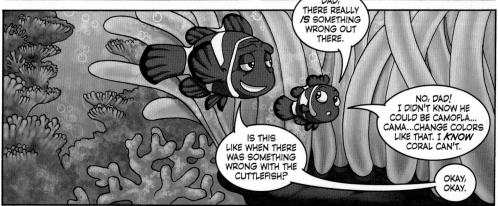

DAD, THERE REALLY *IS* SOMETHING WRONG OUT THERE.

NO, DAD! I DIDN'T KNOW HE COULD BE CAMOFLA... CAMA...CHANGE COLORS LIKE THAT. I *KNOW* CORAL CAN'T.

IS THIS LIKE WHEN THERE WAS SOMETHING WRONG WITH THE CUTTLEFISH?

OKAY, OKAY.

SO THE CORAL IS TURNING COLOR?

≷YAWN≶ UN-HUH...IT LOOKS *REALLY SICK,* DAD. IT WAS KIND OF SCARY. WHY WOULD IT BE GRAY?

I DON'T KNOW.

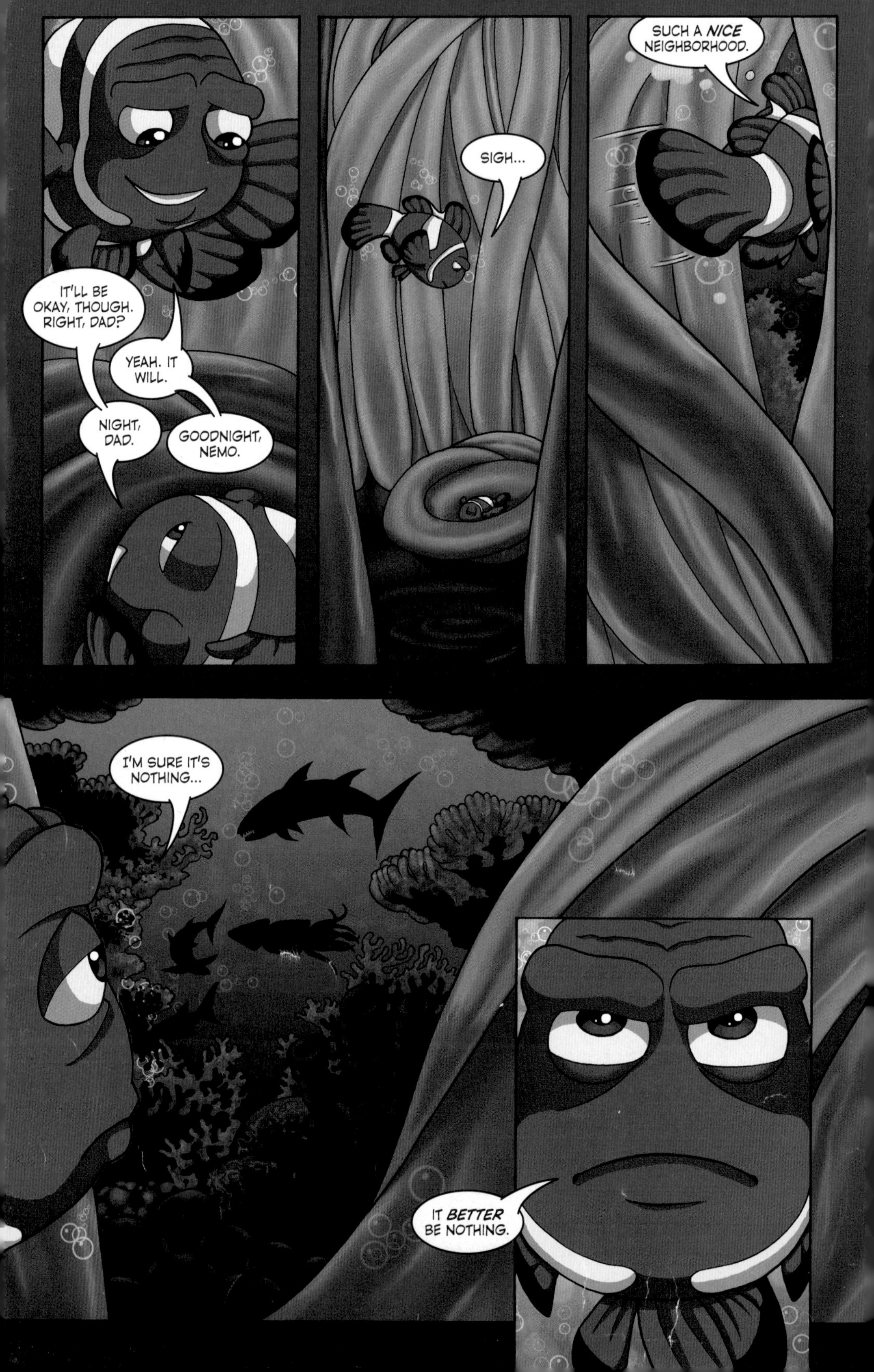
IT'LL BE OKAY, THOUGH. RIGHT, DAD?
YEAH. IT WILL.
NIGHT, DAD.
GOODNIGHT, NEMO.
SIGH...
SUCH A NICE NEIGHBORHOOD.
I'M SURE IT'S NOTHING...
IT BETTER BE NOTHING.

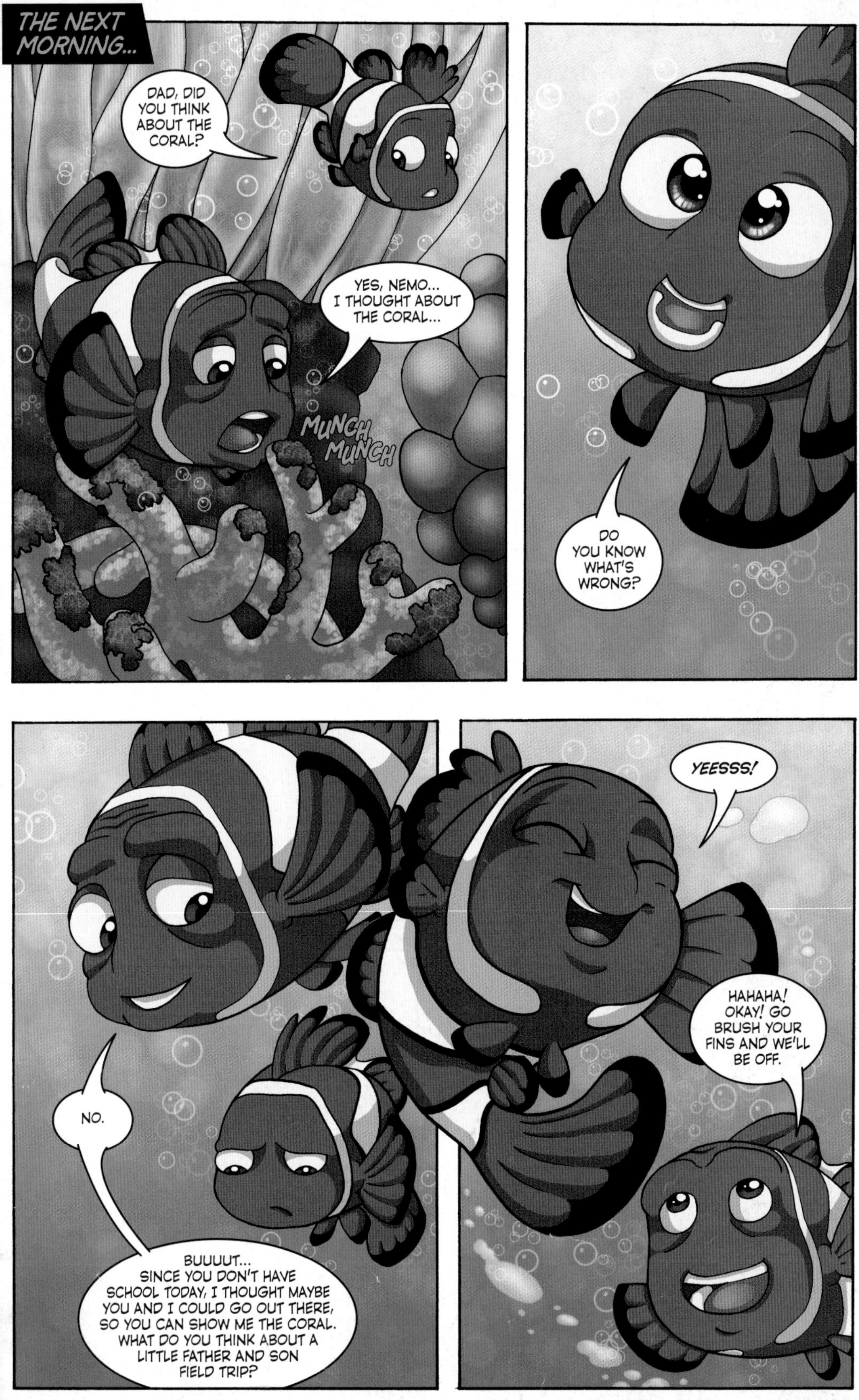
THE NEXT MORNING...
DAD, DID YOU THINK ABOUT THE CORAL?
YES, NEMO... I THOUGHT ABOUT THE CORAL...
MUNCH MUNCH
DO YOU KNOW WHAT'S WRONG?
NO.
BUUUUT... SINCE YOU DON'T HAVE SCHOOL TODAY, I THOUGHT MAYBE YOU AND I COULD GO OUT THERE, SO YOU CAN SHOW ME THE CORAL. WHAT DO YOU THINK ABOUT A LITTLE FATHER AND SON FIELD TRIP?
YEESSS!
HAHAHA! OKAY! GO BRUSH YOUR FINS AND WE'LL BE OFF.

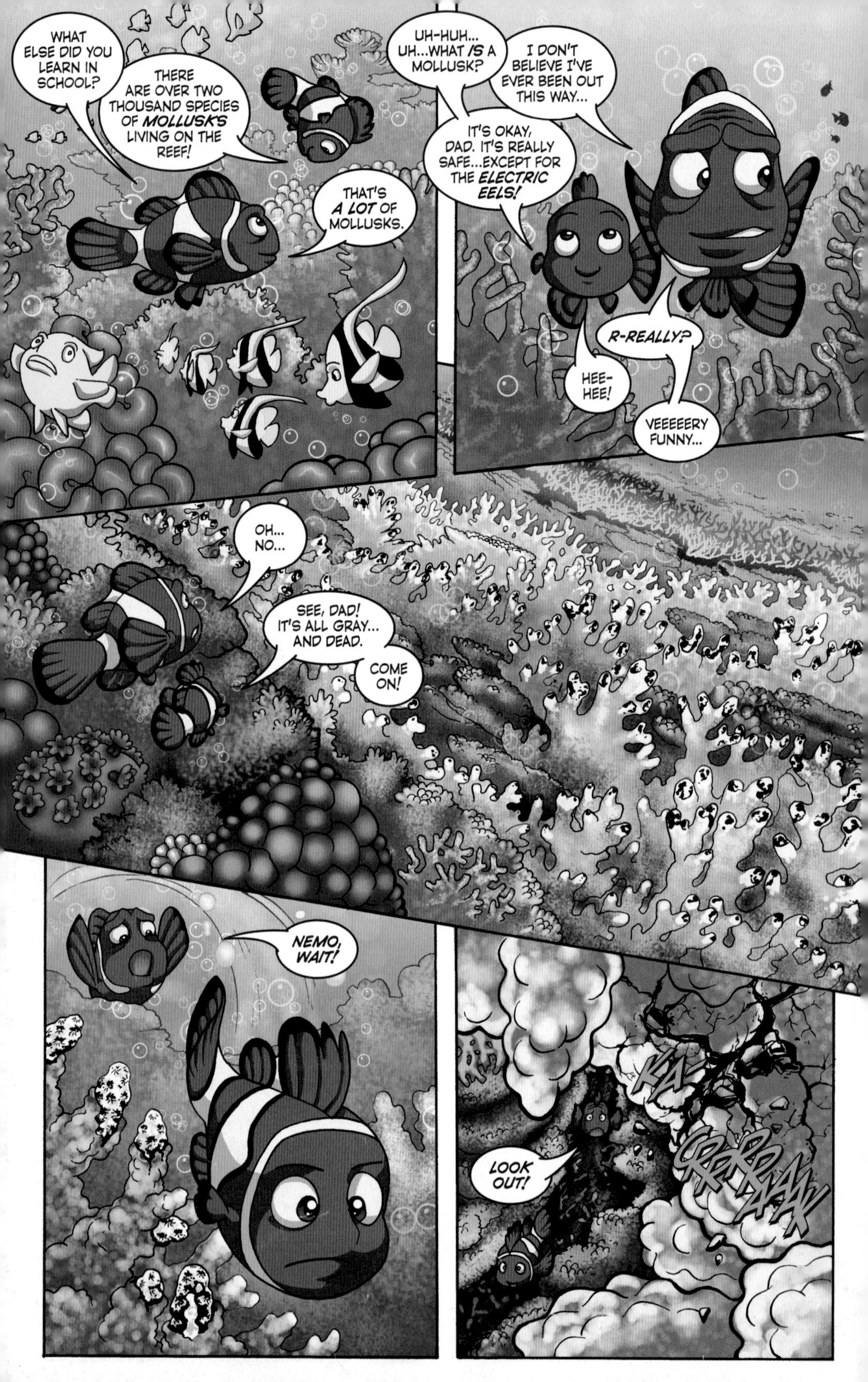
WHAT ELSE DID YOU LEARN IN SCHOOL?
THERE ARE OVER TWO THOUSAND SPECIES OF MOLLUSKS LIVING ON THE REEF!
THAT'S A LOT OF MOLLUSKS.
UH-HUH... UH...WHAT IS A MOLLUSK?
I DON'T BELIEVE I'VE EVER BEEN OUT THIS WAY...
IT'S OKAY, DAD. IT'S REALLY SAFE...EXCEPT FOR THE ELECTRIC EELS!
R-REALLY?
HEE-HEE!
VEEEEERY FUNNY...
OH... NO...
SEE, DAD! IT'S ALL GRAY... AND DEAD.
COME ON!
NEMO, WAIT!
KA-
LOOK OUT!
CRRRAAAK

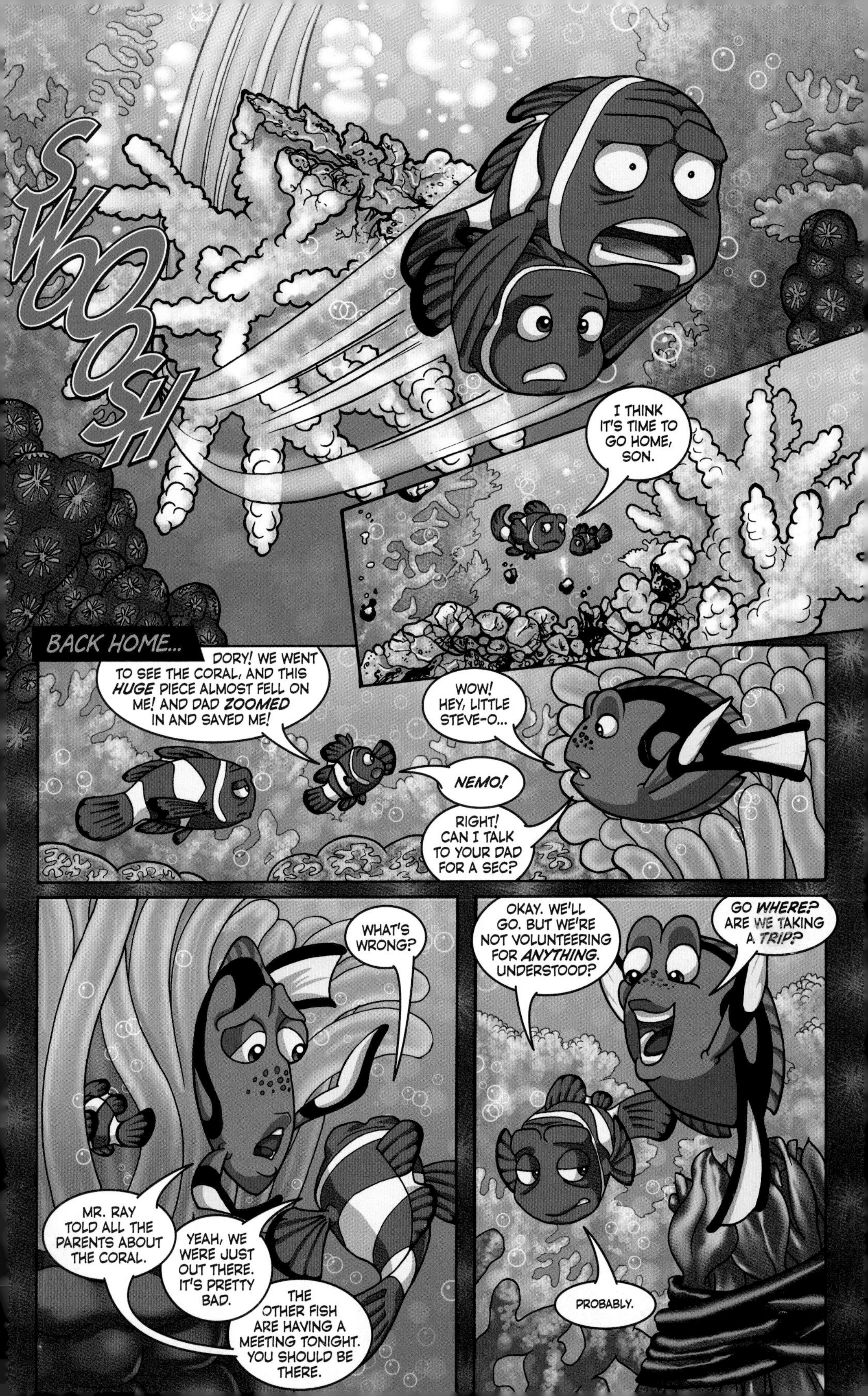
SWOOOSH
I THINK IT'S TIME TO GO HOME, SON.
BACK HOME...
DORY! WE WENT TO SEE THE CORAL, AND THIS HUGE PIECE ALMOST FELL ON ME! AND DAD ZOOMED IN AND SAVED ME!
WOW! HEY, LITTLE STEVE-O...
NEMO!
RIGHT! CAN I TALK TO YOUR DAD FOR A SEC?
WHAT'S WRONG?
MR. RAY TOLD ALL THE PARENTS ABOUT THE CORAL.
YEAH, WE WERE JUST OUT THERE. IT'S PRETTY BAD.
THE OTHER FISH ARE HAVING A MEETING TONIGHT. YOU SHOULD BE THERE.
OKAY. WE'LL GO. BUT WE'RE NOT VOLUNTEERING FOR ANYTHING. UNDERSTOOD?
GO WHERE? ARE WE TAKING A TRIP?
PROBABLY.

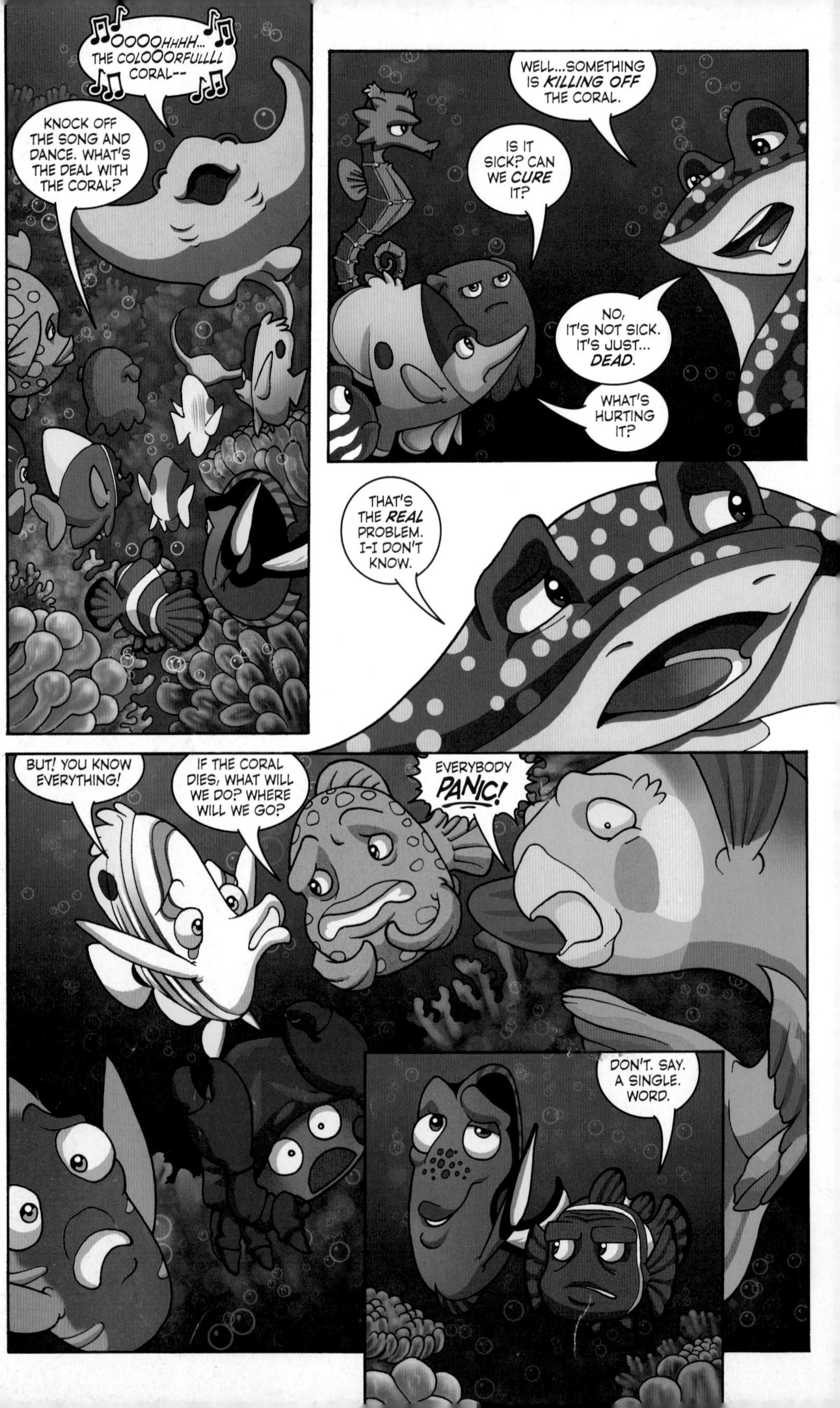
OOOOHHHH... THE COLOOORFULLLL CORAL--
KNOCK OFF THE SONG AND DANCE. WHAT'S THE DEAL WITH THE CORAL?
WELL...SOMETHING IS KILLING OFF THE CORAL.
IS IT SICK? CAN WE CURE IT?
NO, IT'S NOT SICK. IT'S JUST... DEAD.
WHAT'S HURTING IT?
THAT'S THE REAL PROBLEM. I-I DON'T KNOW.
BUT! YOU KNOW EVERYTHING!
IF THE CORAL DIES, WHAT WILL WE DO? WHERE WILL WE GO?
EVERYBODY PANIC!
DON'T. SAY. A SINGLE. WORD.

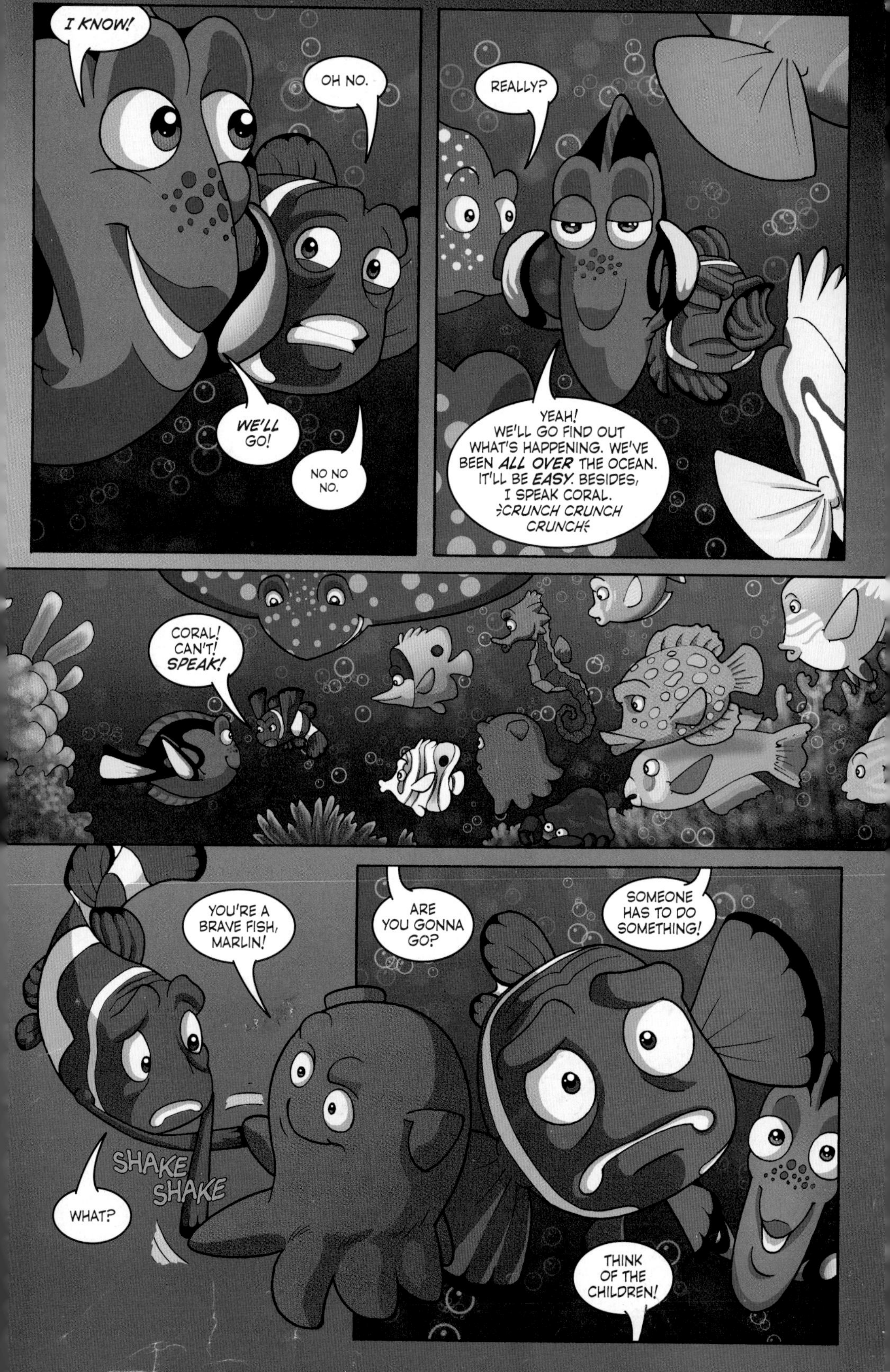
I KNOW!
OH NO.
WE'LL GO!
NO NO NO.
REALLY?
YEAH! WE'LL GO FIND OUT WHAT'S HAPPENING. WE'VE BEEN ALL OVER THE OCEAN. IT'LL BE EASY. BESIDES, I SPEAK CORAL. CRUNCH CRUNCH CRUNCH
CORAL! CAN'T! SPEAK!
YOU'RE A BRAVE FISH, MARLIN!
ARE YOU GONNA GO?
SOMEONE HAS TO DO SOMETHING!
WHAT?
SHAKE SHAKE
THINK OF THE CHILDREN!

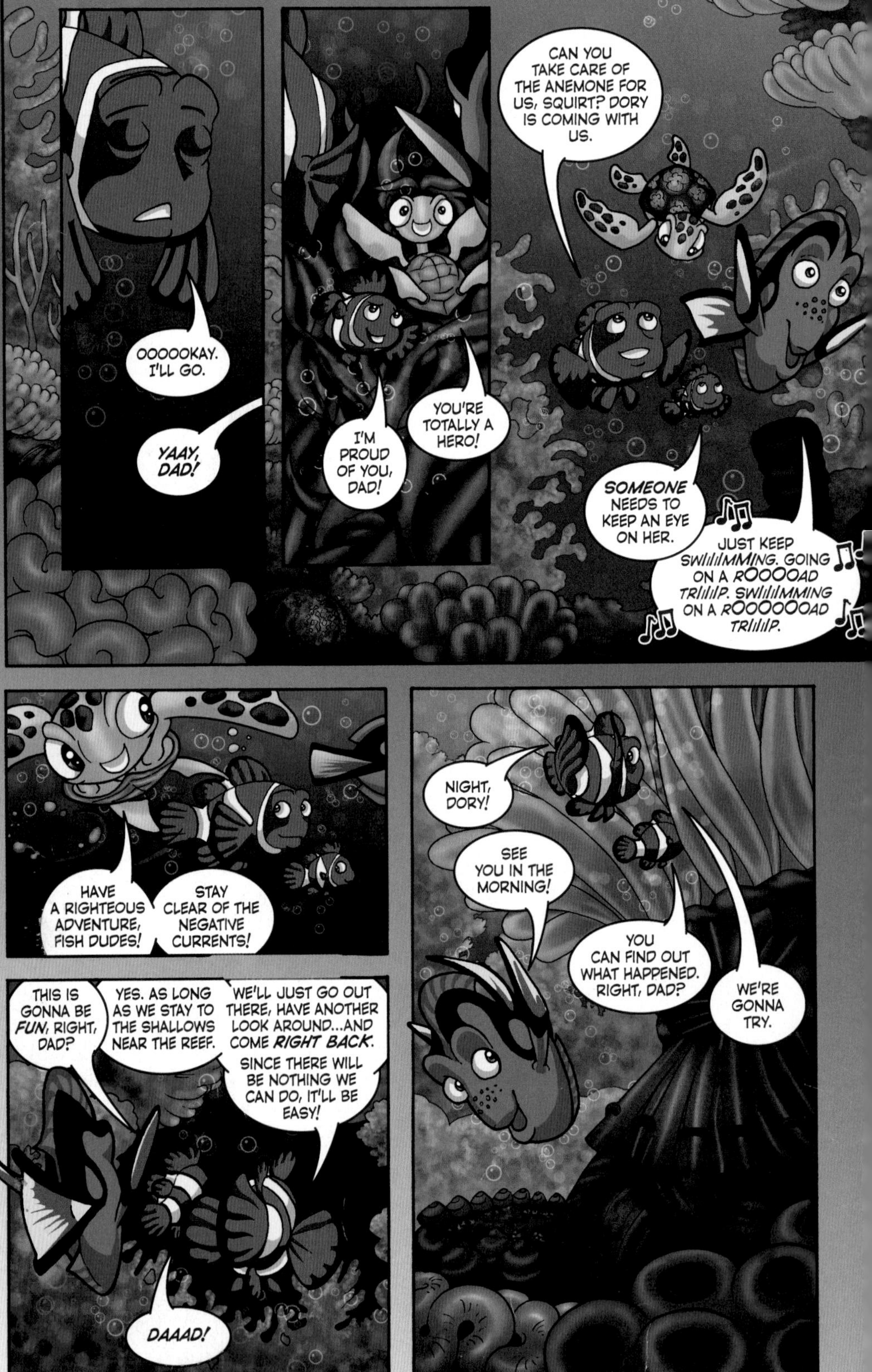
OOOOOKAY. I'LL GO.
YAAY, DAD!
I'M PROUD OF YOU, DAD!
YOU'RE TOTALLY A HERO!
CAN YOU TAKE CARE OF THE ANEMONE FOR US, SQUIRT? DORY IS COMING WITH US.
SOMEONE NEEDS TO KEEP AN EYE ON HER.
JUST KEEP SWIIIIMMING. GOING ON A ROOOOAD TRIIIIP. SWIIIIMMING ON A ROOOOOOAD TRIIIIP.
HAVE A RIGHTEOUS ADVENTURE, FISH DUDES!
STAY CLEAR OF THE NEGATIVE CURRENTS!
NIGHT, DORY!
SEE YOU IN THE MORNING!
YOU CAN FIND OUT WHAT HAPPENED. RIGHT, DAD?
WE'RE GONNA TRY.
THIS IS GONNA BE FUN, RIGHT, DAD?
YES. AS LONG AS WE STAY TO THE SHALLOWS NEAR THE REEF.
WE'LL JUST GO OUT THERE, HAVE ANOTHER LOOK AROUND...AND COME RIGHT BACK.
SINCE THERE WILL BE NOTHING WE CAN DO, IT'LL BE EASY!
DAAAD!

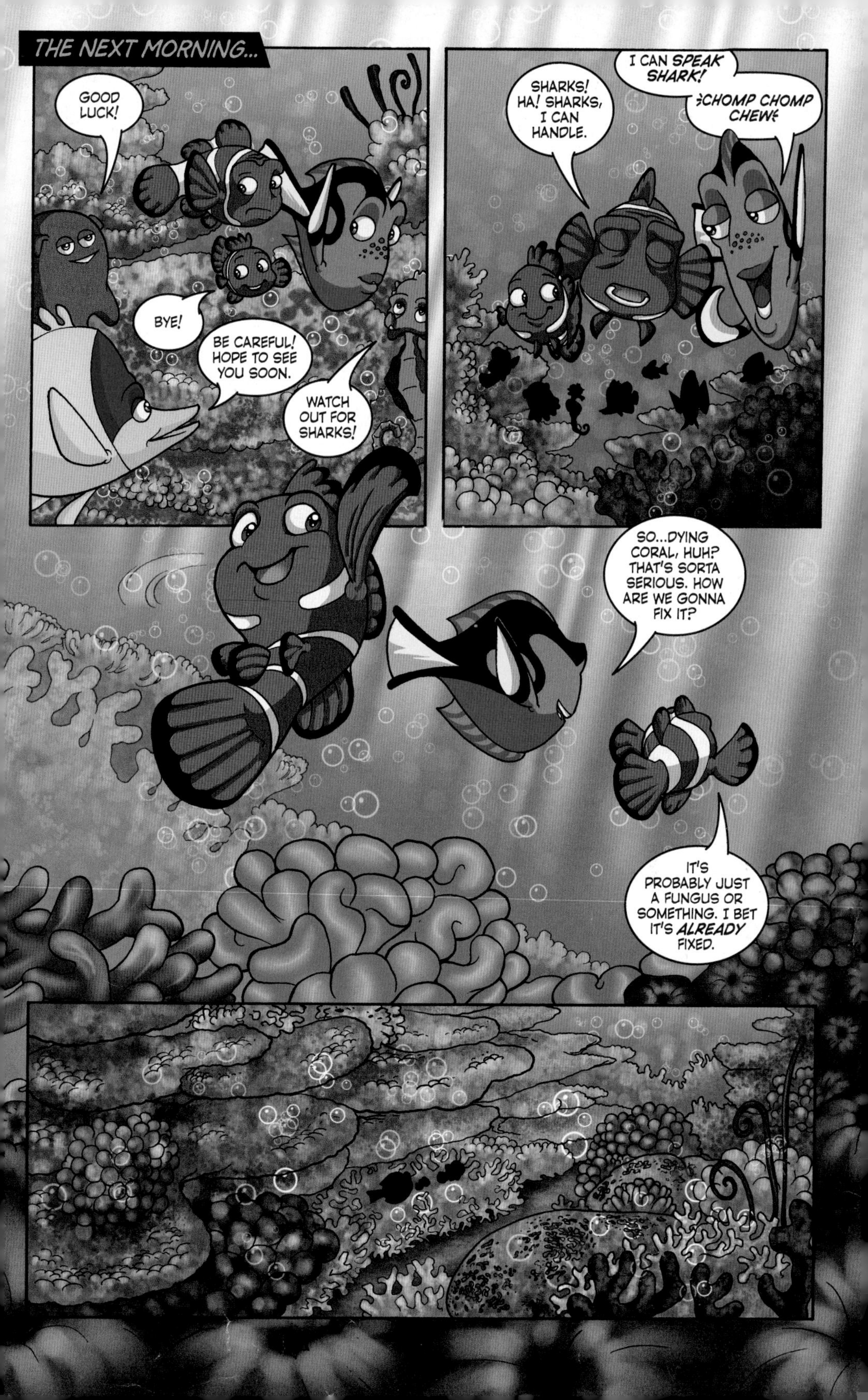
THE NEXT MORNING...
GOOD LUCK!
BYE!
BE CAREFUL! HOPE TO SEE YOU SOON.
WATCH OUT FOR SHARKS!
SHARKS! HA! SHARKS, I CAN HANDLE.
I CAN SPEAK SHARK!
CHOMP CHOMP CHEW
SO...DYING CORAL, HUH? THAT'S SORTA SERIOUS. HOW ARE WE GONNA FIX IT?
IT'S PROBABLY JUST A FUNGUS OR SOMETHING. I BET IT'S ALREADY FIXED.

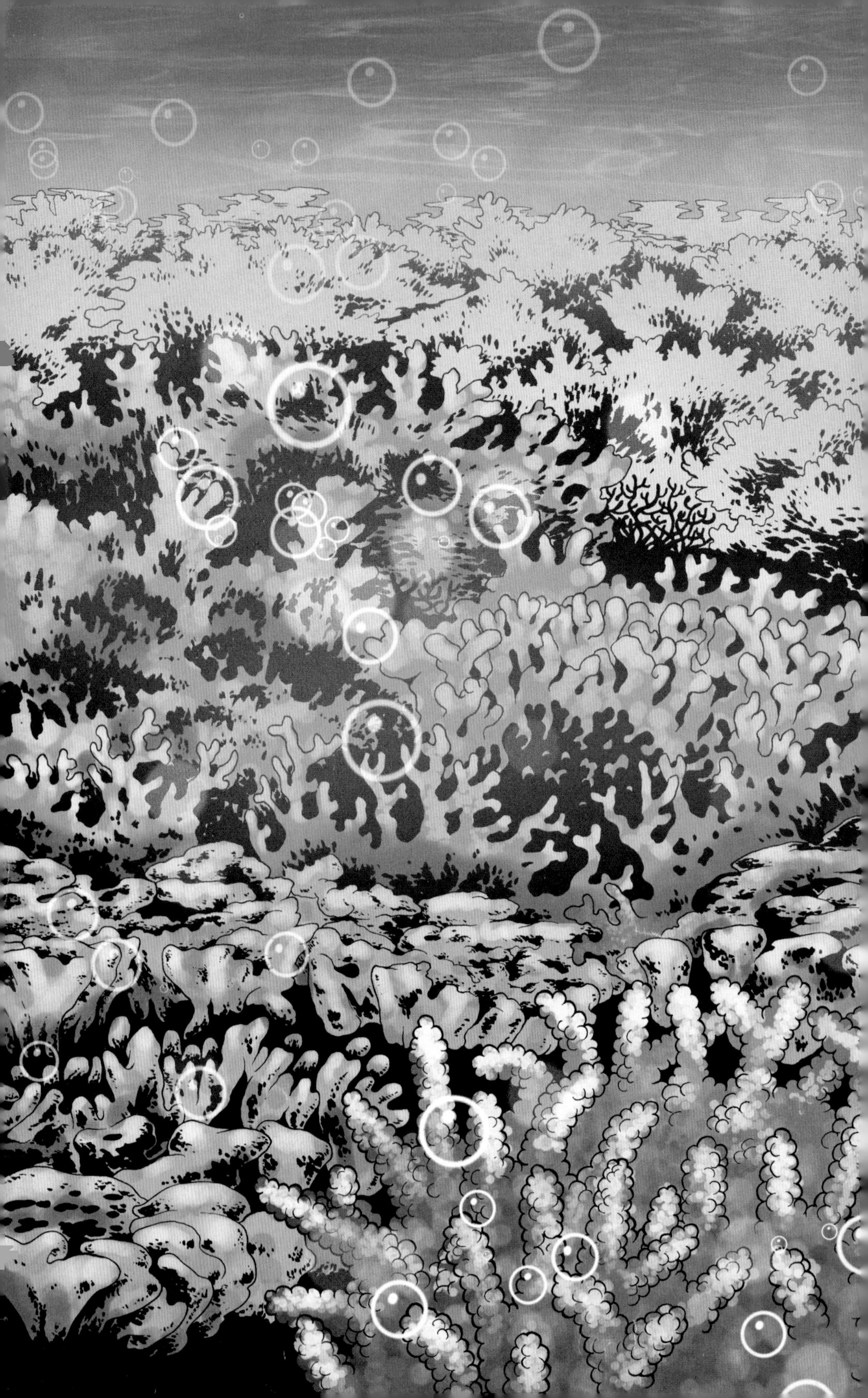

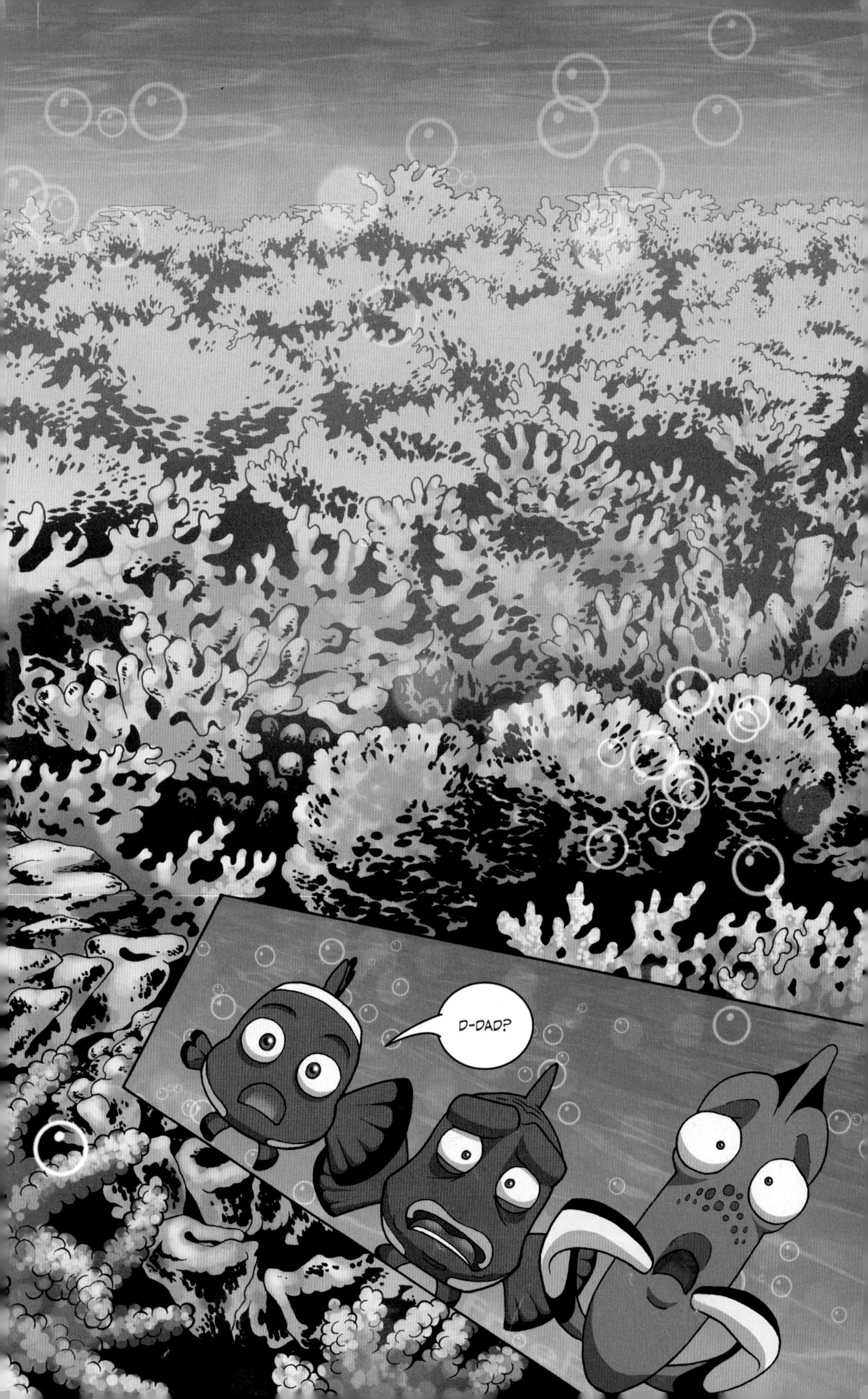
D-DAD?

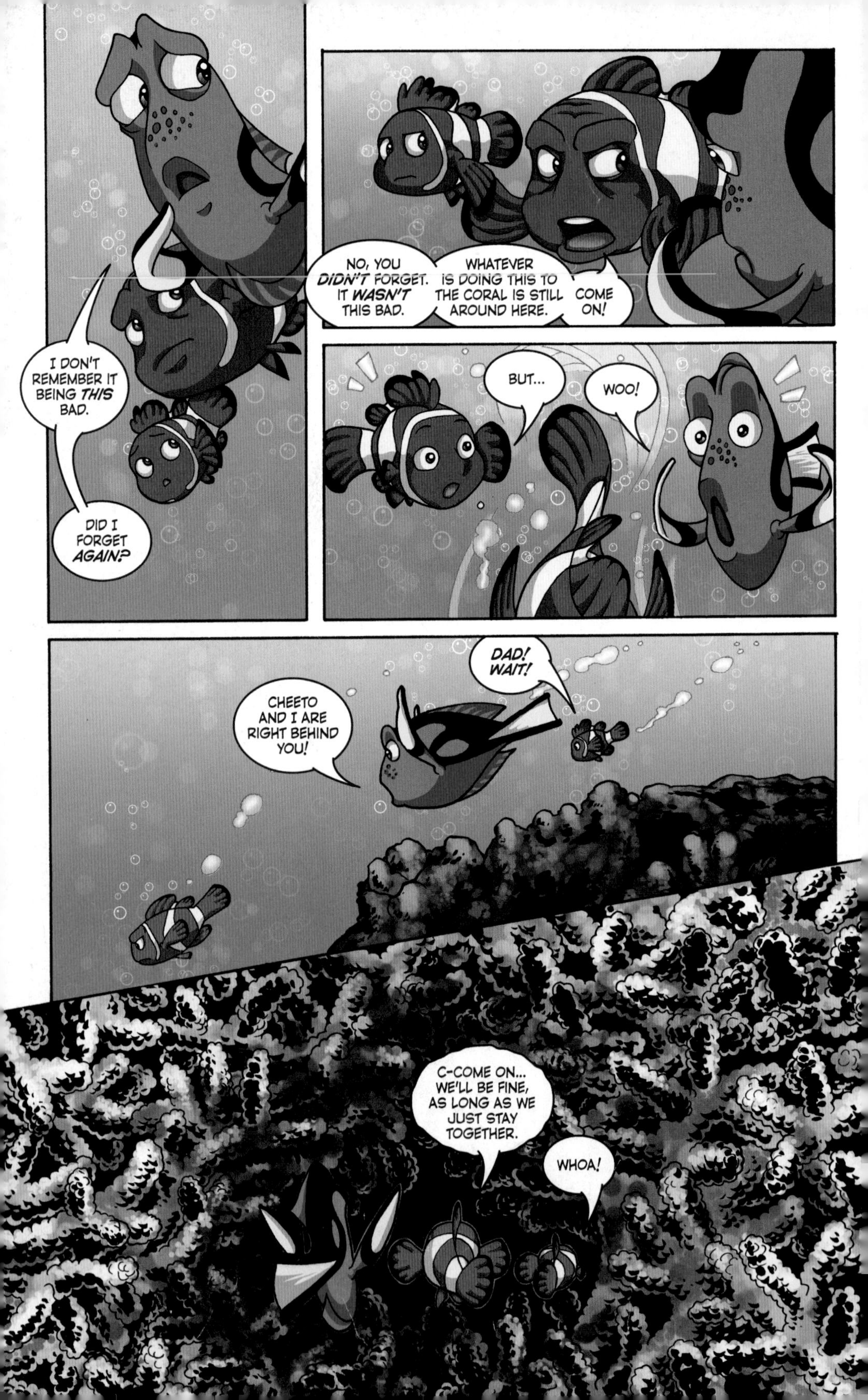
I DON'T REMEMBER IT BEING THIS BAD.
DID I FORGET AGAIN?
NO, YOU DIDN'T FORGET. IT WASN'T THIS BAD.
WHATEVER IS DOING THIS TO THE CORAL IS STILL AROUND HERE.
COME ON!
BUT...
WOO!
DAD! WAIT!
CHEETO AND I ARE RIGHT BEHIND YOU!
C-COME ON... WE'LL BE FINE, AS LONG AS WE JUST STAY TOGETHER.
WHOA!

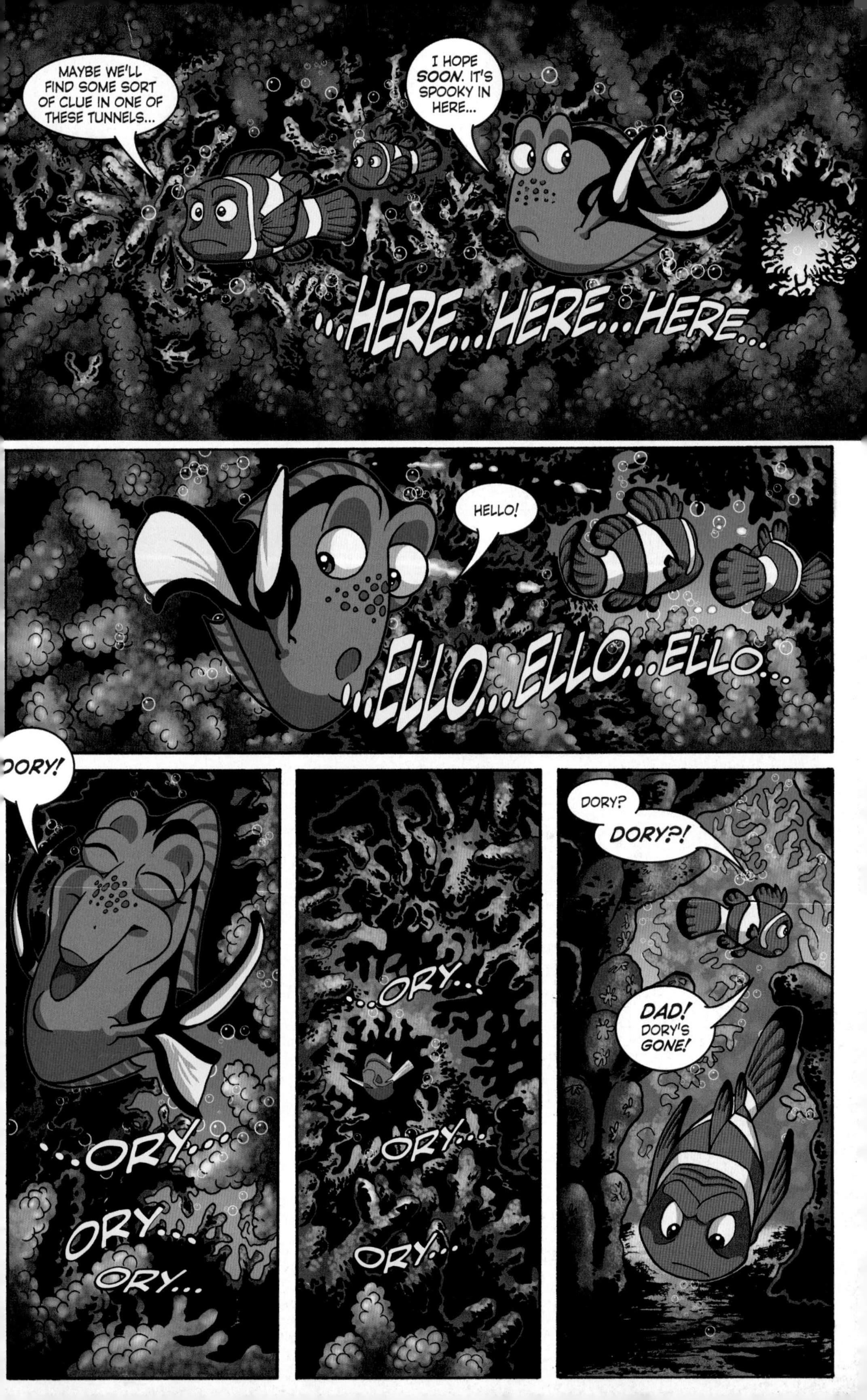

MAYBE WE'LL FIND SOME SORT OF CLUE IN ONE OF THESE TUNNELS...
I HOPE SOON. IT'S SPOOKY IN HERE...
...HERE...HERE...HERE...
HELLO!
...ELLO...ELLO...ELLO...
DORY!
...ORY...
ORY...
ORY...
...ORY...
ORY...
ORY...
DORY?
DORY?!
DAD! DORY'S GONE!

WHY CAN'T SHE EVER STAY OUT OF TROUBLE?

COME ON!

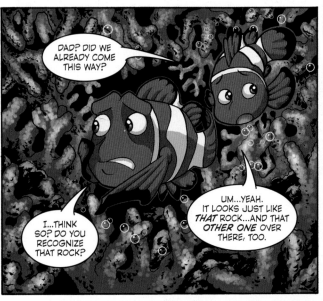

DAD? DID WE ALREADY COME THIS WAY?

I...THINK SO? DO YOU RECOGNIZE THAT ROCK?

UM...YEAH. IT LOOKS JUST LIKE *THAT* ROCK...AND THAT *OTHER ONE* OVER THERE, TOO.

FUNNY. BUT *NOT* HELPFUL.

DAD, DO YOU HEAR THAT?

...ORY...

ORY...

ORY...

*THIS WAY!*

...ORY...

WE'RE COMING, DORY!

ORY...

ORY...

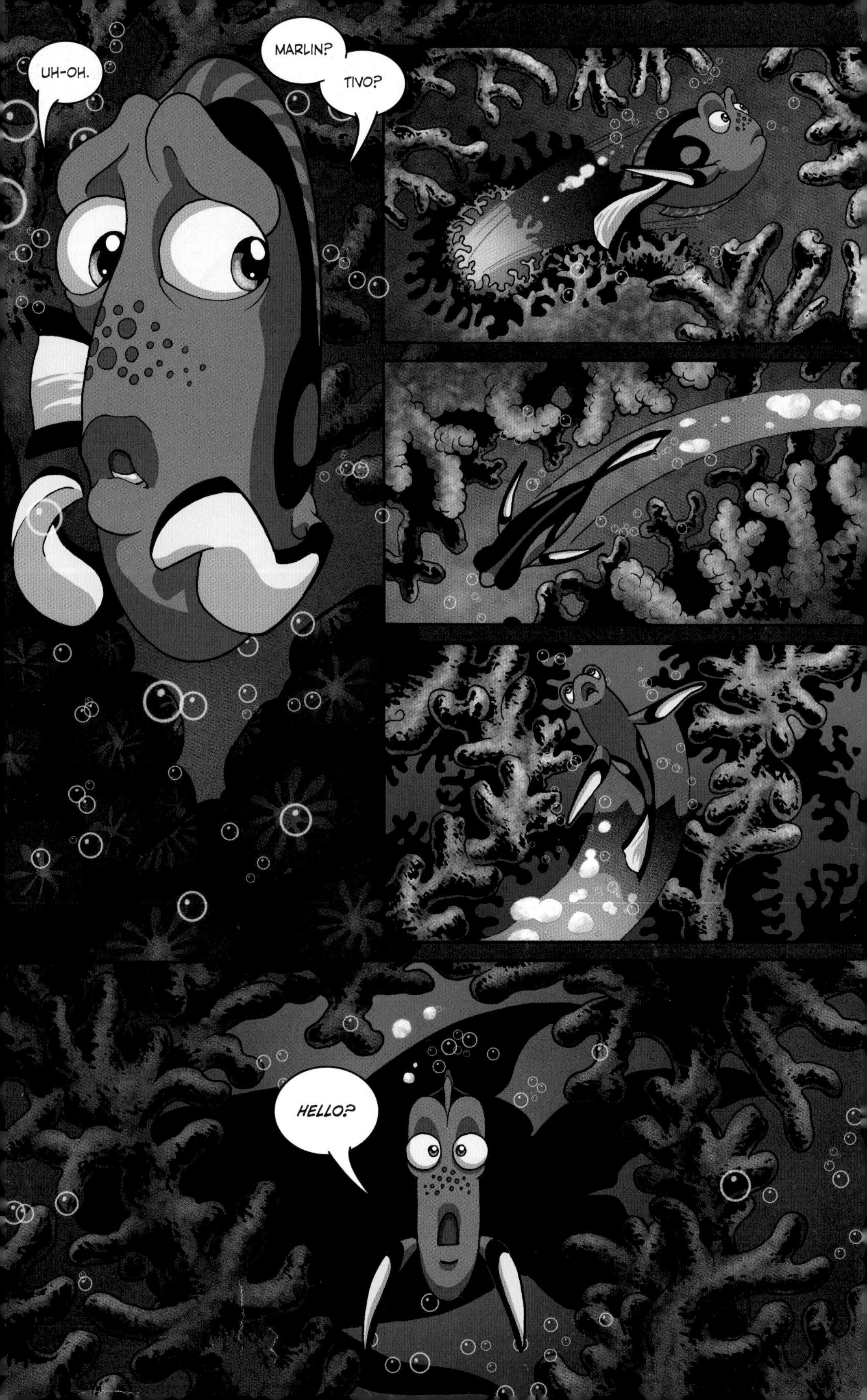
UH-OH.
MARLIN?
TIVO?
HELLO?

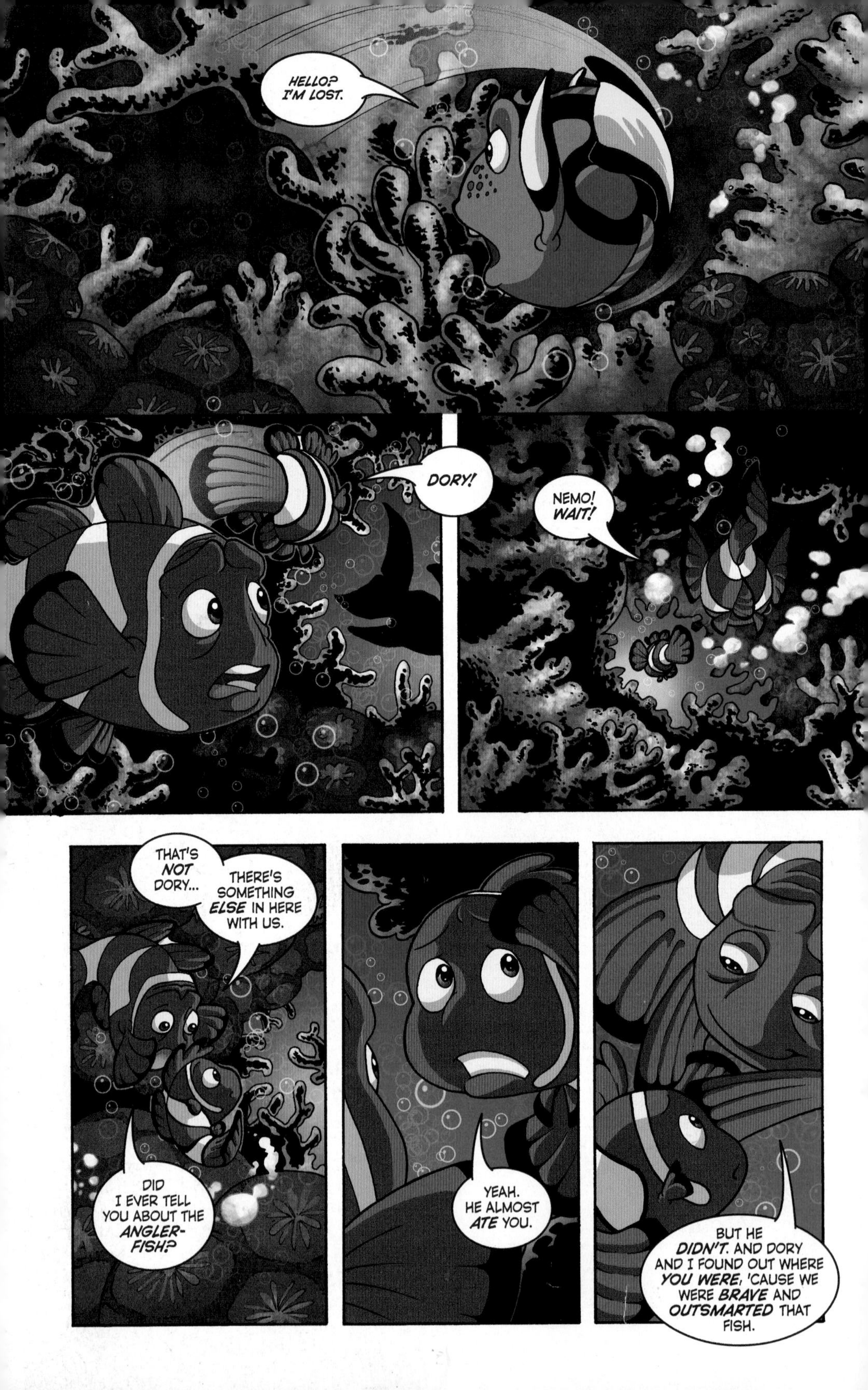
HELLO? I'M LOST.
DORY!
NEMO! WAIT!
THAT'S NOT DORY...
THERE'S SOMETHING ELSE IN HERE WITH US.
DID I EVER TELL YOU ABOUT THE ANGLER-FISH?
YEAH. HE ALMOST ATE YOU.
BUT HE DIDN'T. AND DORY AND I FOUND OUT WHERE YOU WERE, 'CAUSE WE WERE BRAVE AND OUTSMARTED THAT FISH.

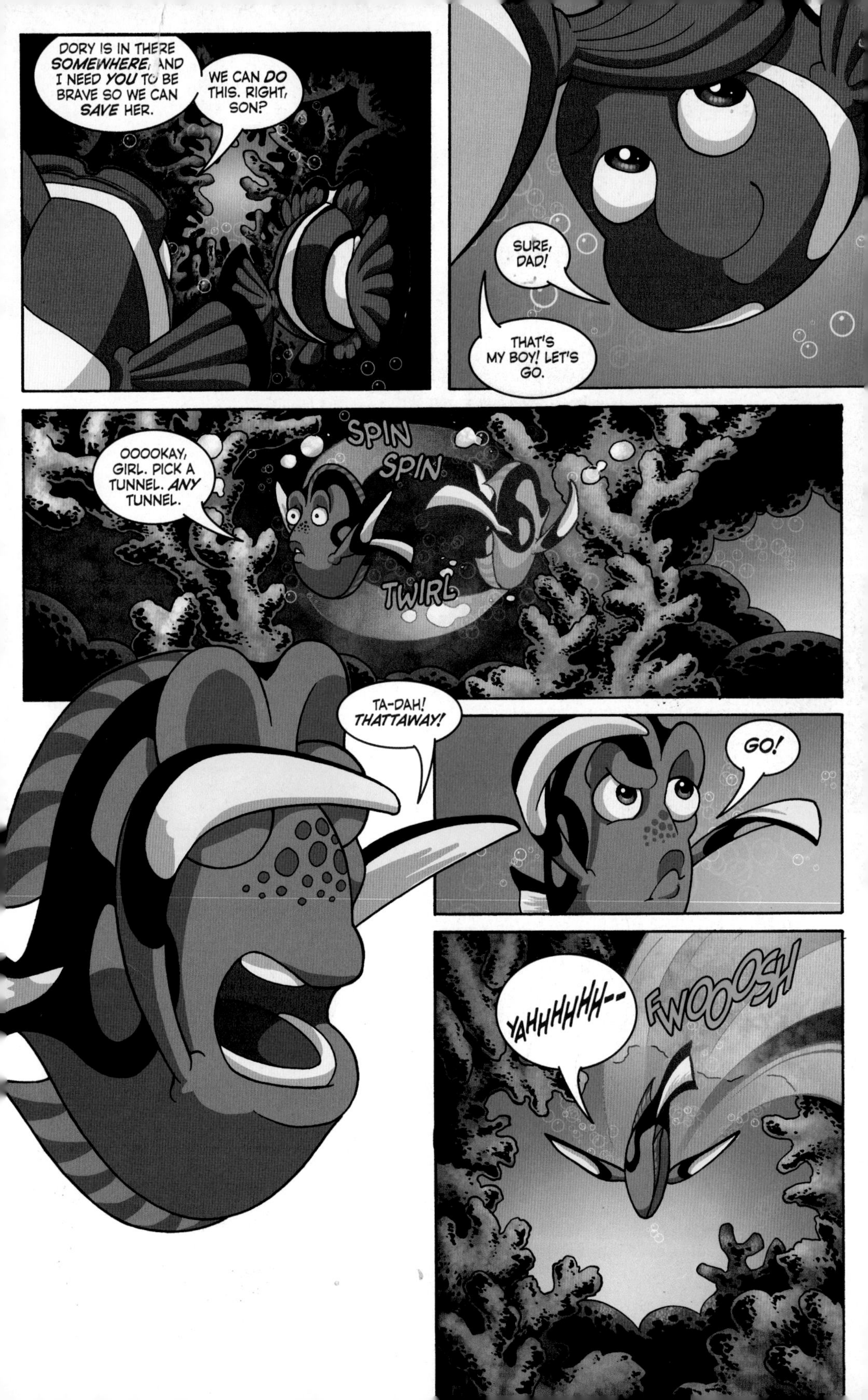
DORY IS IN THERE SOMEWHERE, AND I NEED YOU TO BE BRAVE SO WE CAN SAVE HER.
WE CAN DO THIS. RIGHT, SON?
SURE, DAD!
THAT'S MY BOY! LET'S GO.
OOOOKAY, GIRL. PICK A TUNNEL. ANY TUNNEL.
SPIN
SPIN
TWIRL
TA-DAH! THATTAWAY!
GO!
YAHHHHHH--
FWOOOSH

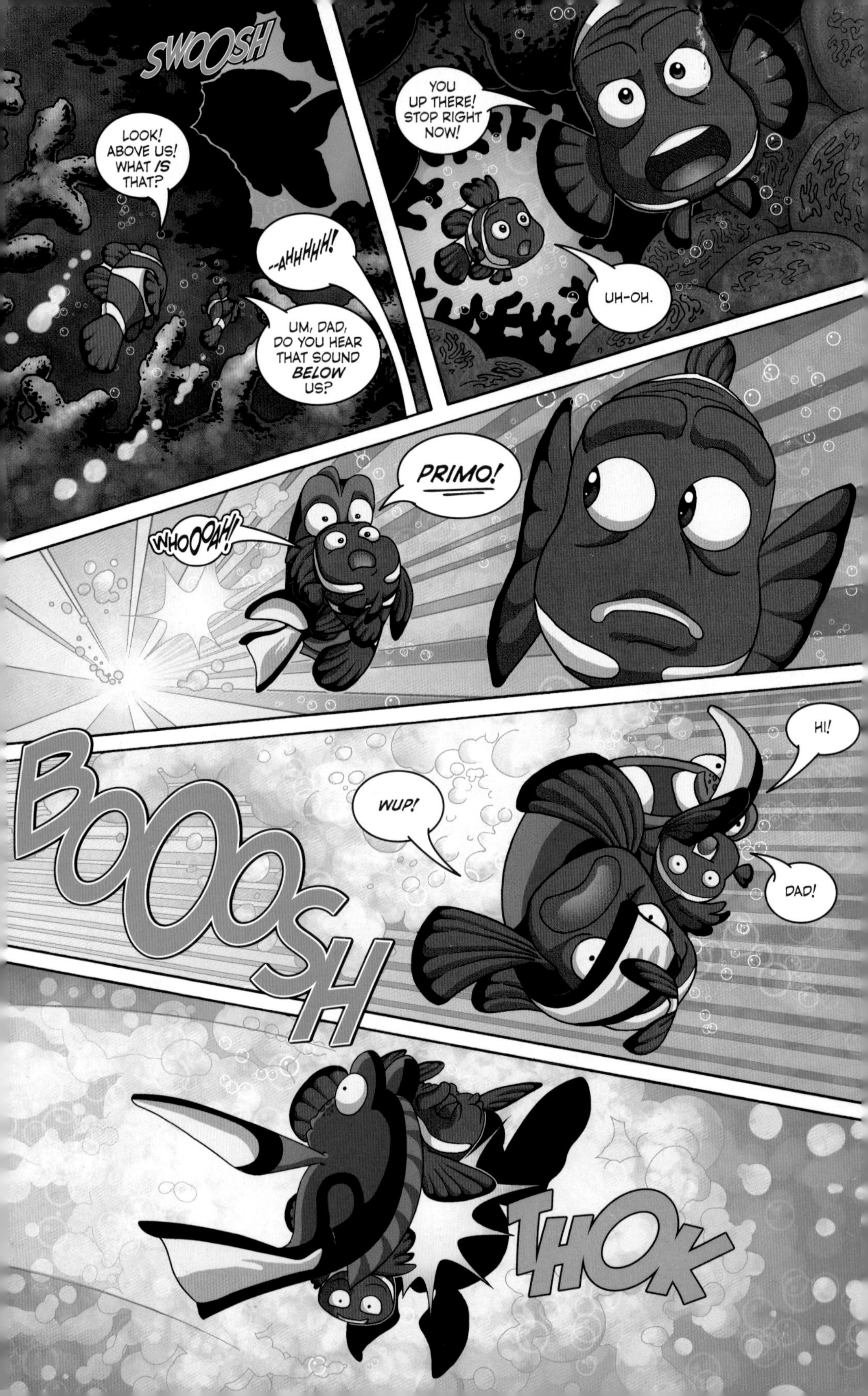
SWOOSH
LOOK! ABOVE US! WHAT IS THAT?
--AHHHHH!
UM, DAD, DO YOU HEAR THAT SOUND BELOW US?
YOU UP THERE! STOP RIGHT NOW!
UH-OH.
WHOOOAH!
PRIMO!
BOOOOSH
WUP!
HI!
DAD!
THOK

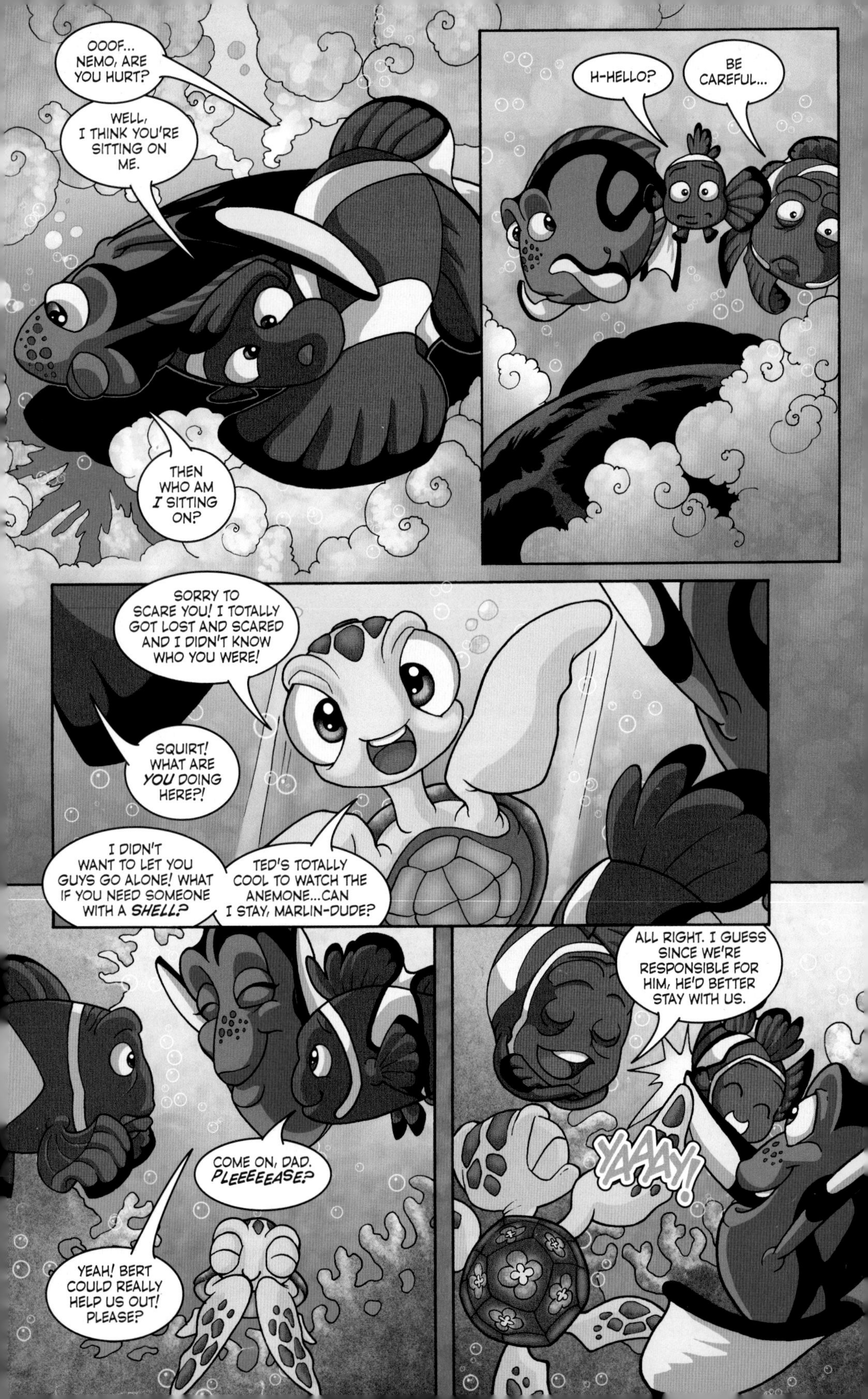
OOOF... NEMO, ARE YOU HURT?
WELL, I THINK YOU'RE SITTING ON ME.
THEN WHO AM *I* SITTING ON?
H-HELLO?
BE CAREFUL...
SORRY TO SCARE YOU! I TOTALLY GOT LOST AND SCARED AND I DIDN'T KNOW WHO YOU WERE!
SQUIRT! WHAT ARE *YOU* DOING HERE?!
I DIDN'T WANT TO LET YOU GUYS GO ALONE! WHAT IF YOU NEED SOMEONE WITH A *SHELL?*
TED'S TOTALLY COOL TO WATCH THE ANEMONE...CAN I STAY, MARLIN-DUDE?
COME ON, DAD. *PLEEEEEASE?*
YEAH! BERT COULD REALLY HELP US OUT! PLEASE?
ALL RIGHT. I GUESS SINCE WE'RE RESPONSIBLE FOR HIM, HE'D BETTER STAY WITH US.
YAAAY!

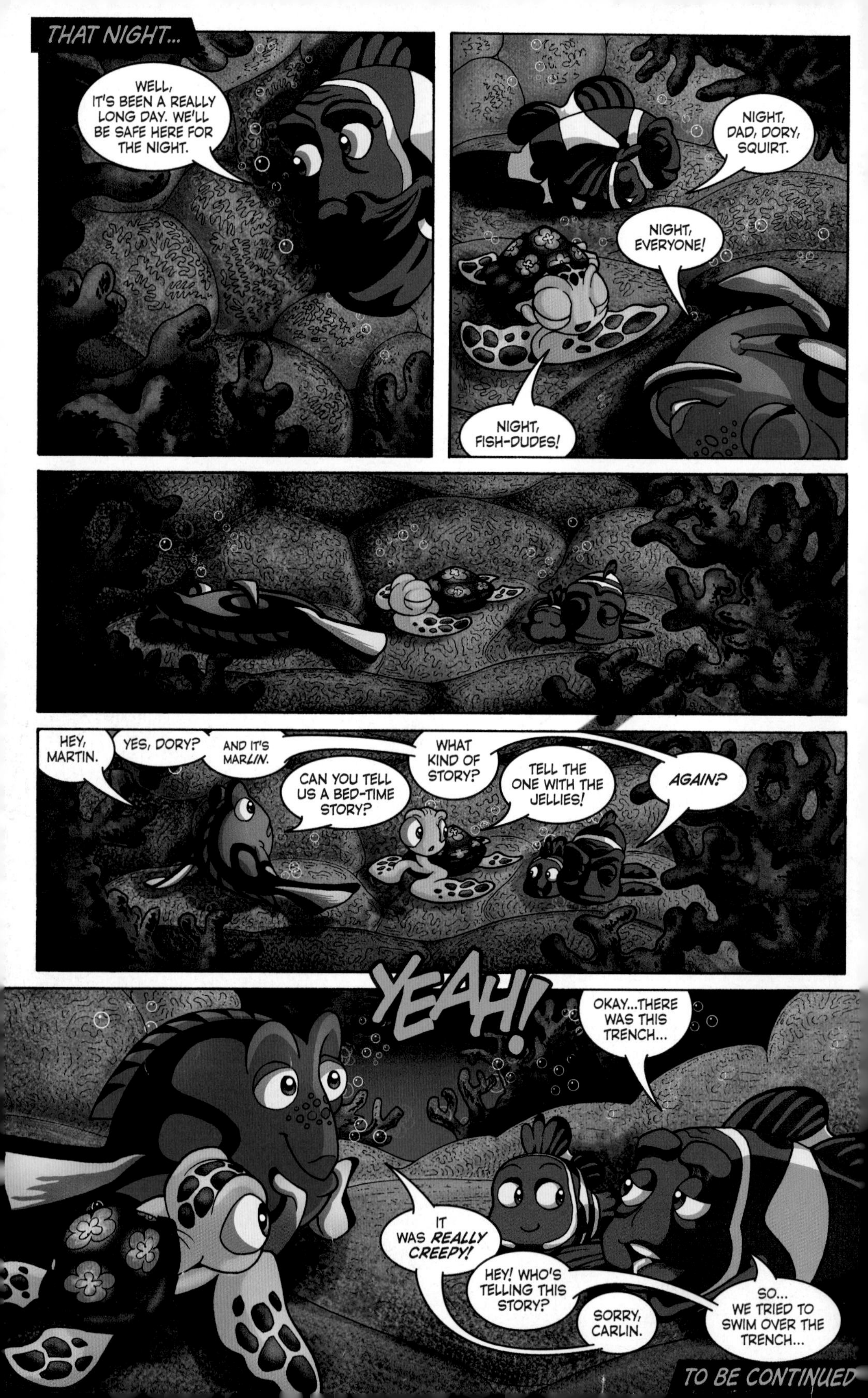
THAT NIGHT...
WELL, IT'S BEEN A REALLY LONG DAY. WE'LL BE SAFE HERE FOR THE NIGHT.
NIGHT, DAD, DORY, SQUIRT.
NIGHT, EVERYONE!
NIGHT, FISH-DUDES!
HEY, MARTIN.
YES, DORY?
AND IT'S MARLIN.
CAN YOU TELL US A BED-TIME STORY?
WHAT KIND OF STORY?
TELL THE ONE WITH THE JELLIES!
AGAIN?
YEAH!
OKAY...THERE WAS THIS TRENCH...
IT WAS REALLY CREEPY!
HEY! WHO'S TELLING THIS STORY?
SORRY, CARLIN.
SO... WE TRIED TO SWIM OVER THE TRENCH...
TO BE CONTINUED

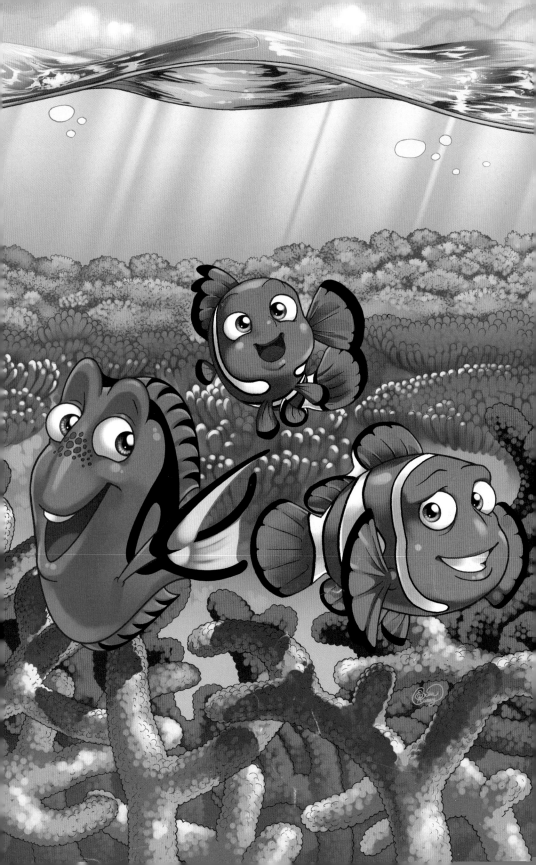

# CHAPTER TWO

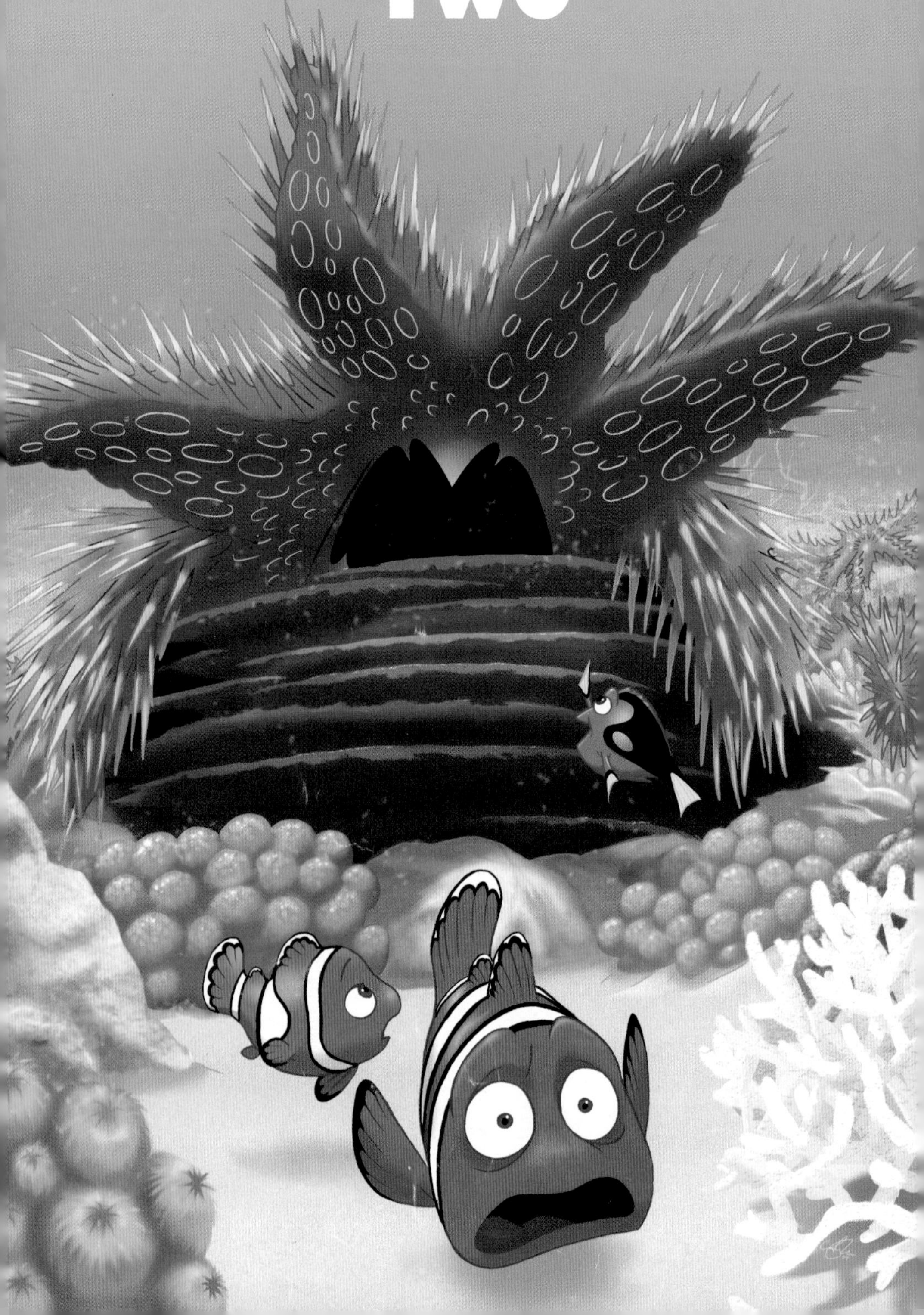

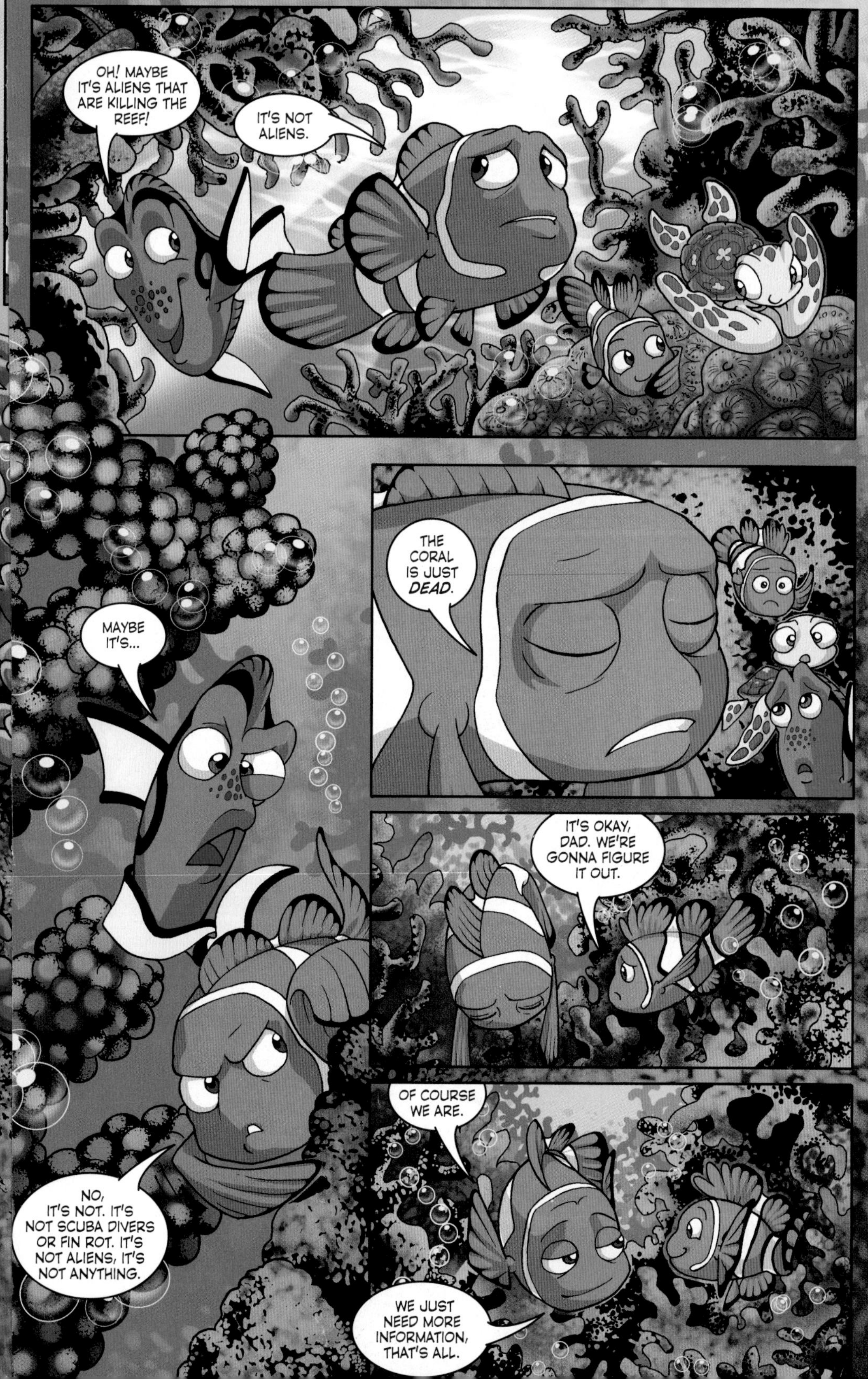
OH! MAYBE IT'S ALIENS THAT ARE KILLING THE REEF!
IT'S NOT ALIENS.
MAYBE IT'S...
NO, IT'S NOT. IT'S NOT SCUBA DIVERS OR FIN ROT. IT'S NOT ALIENS, IT'S NOT ANYTHING.
THE CORAL IS JUST *DEAD*.
IT'S OKAY, DAD. WE'RE GONNA FIGURE IT OUT.
OF COURSE WE ARE.
WE JUST NEED MORE INFORMATION, THAT'S ALL.

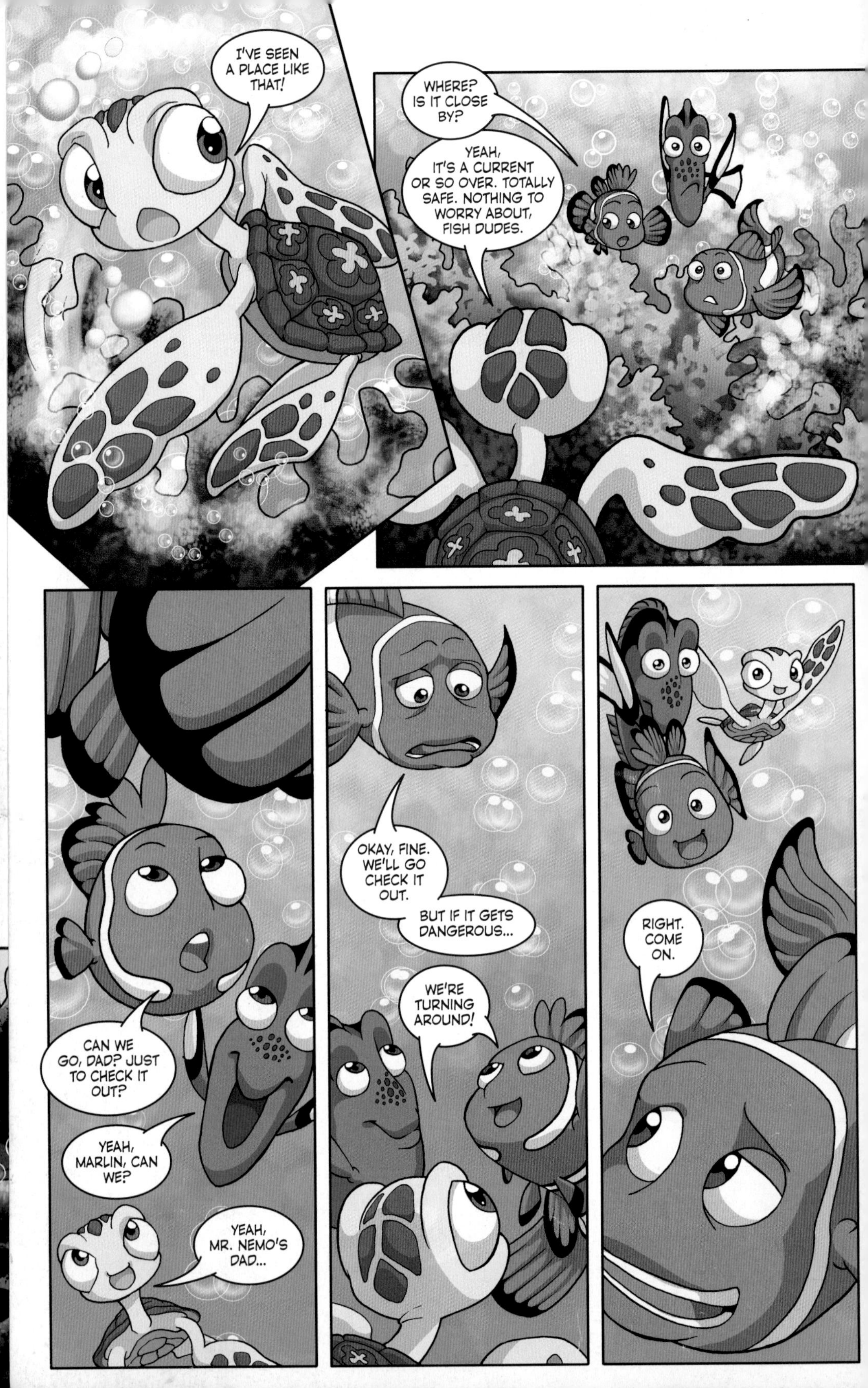
I'VE SEEN A PLACE LIKE THAT!
WHERE? IS IT CLOSE BY?
YEAH, IT'S A CURRENT OR SO OVER. TOTALLY SAFE. NOTHING TO WORRY ABOUT, FISH DUDES.
CAN WE GO, DAD? JUST TO CHECK IT OUT?
YEAH, MARLIN, CAN WE?
YEAH, MR. NEMO'S DAD...
OKAY, FINE. WE'LL GO CHECK IT OUT.
BUT IF IT GETS DANGEROUS...
WE'RE TURNING AROUND!
RIGHT. COME ON.

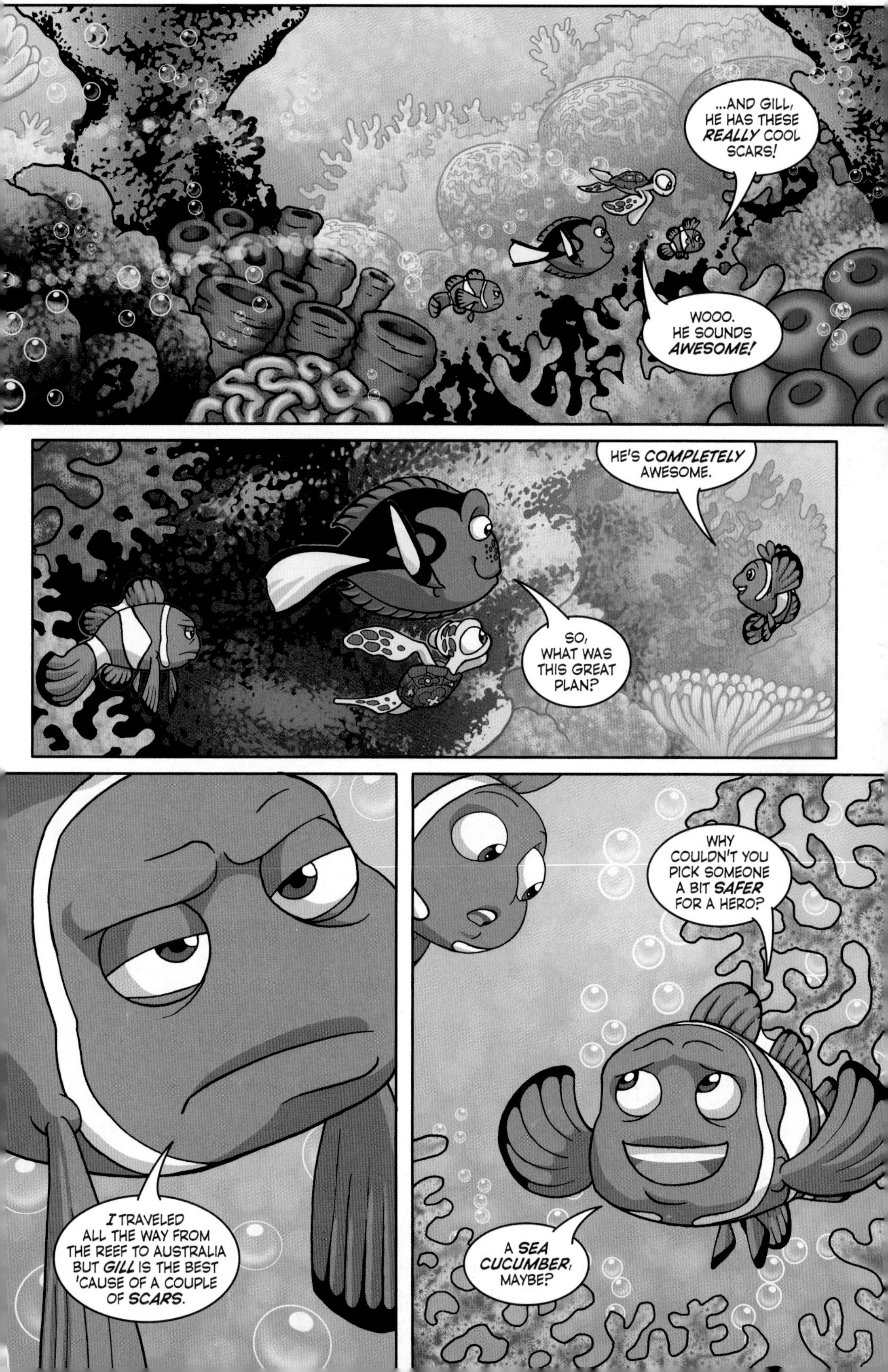
...AND GILL, HE HAS THESE *REALLY* COOL SCARS!
WOOO. HE SOUNDS *AWESOME!*
HE'S *COMPLETELY* AWESOME.
SO, WHAT WAS THIS GREAT PLAN?
*I* TRAVELED ALL THE WAY FROM THE REEF TO AUSTRALIA BUT *GILL* IS THE BEST 'CAUSE OF A COUPLE OF *SCARS*.
WHY COULDN'T YOU PICK SOMEONE A BIT *SAFER* FOR A HERO?
A *SEA CUCUMBER*, MAYBE?

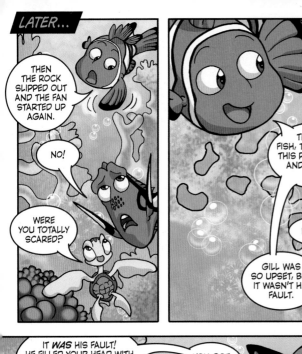

THEN THE ROCK SLIPPED OUT AND THE FAN STARTED UP AGAIN.

NO!

WERE YOU TOTALLY SCARED?

OH YEAH, I REALLY THOUGHT I WAS GONNA GET SUCKED INTO THE FAN.

WHAT HAPPENED THEN?

THE OTHER FISH, THEY GRABBED THIS PLASTIC PLANT AND PULLED ME OUT.

RADICAL!

GILL WAS SO UPSET, BUT IT WASN'T HIS FAULT.

IT *WAS* HIS FAULT! HE FILLED YOUR HEAD WITH ALL OF HIS CRAZY PLANS! HE COULD HAVE GOTTEN YOU KILLED.

YOU GOT LUCKY.

BUT HE DIDN'T, AND HIS PLAN WORKED! SORT OF.

YOU PUT TO MUCH FAITH IN THIS GILL CHARACTER! I JUST DON'T WANT YOU TO BE DISAPPOINTED!

WHY WOULD I BE DISAPPOINTED?

WELL... WE MIGHT NOT BE ABLE TO FIND HIM.

HE MIGHT NOT KNOW HOW TO HELP.

OR HE MIGHT HAVE BEEN EATEN BY EELS!

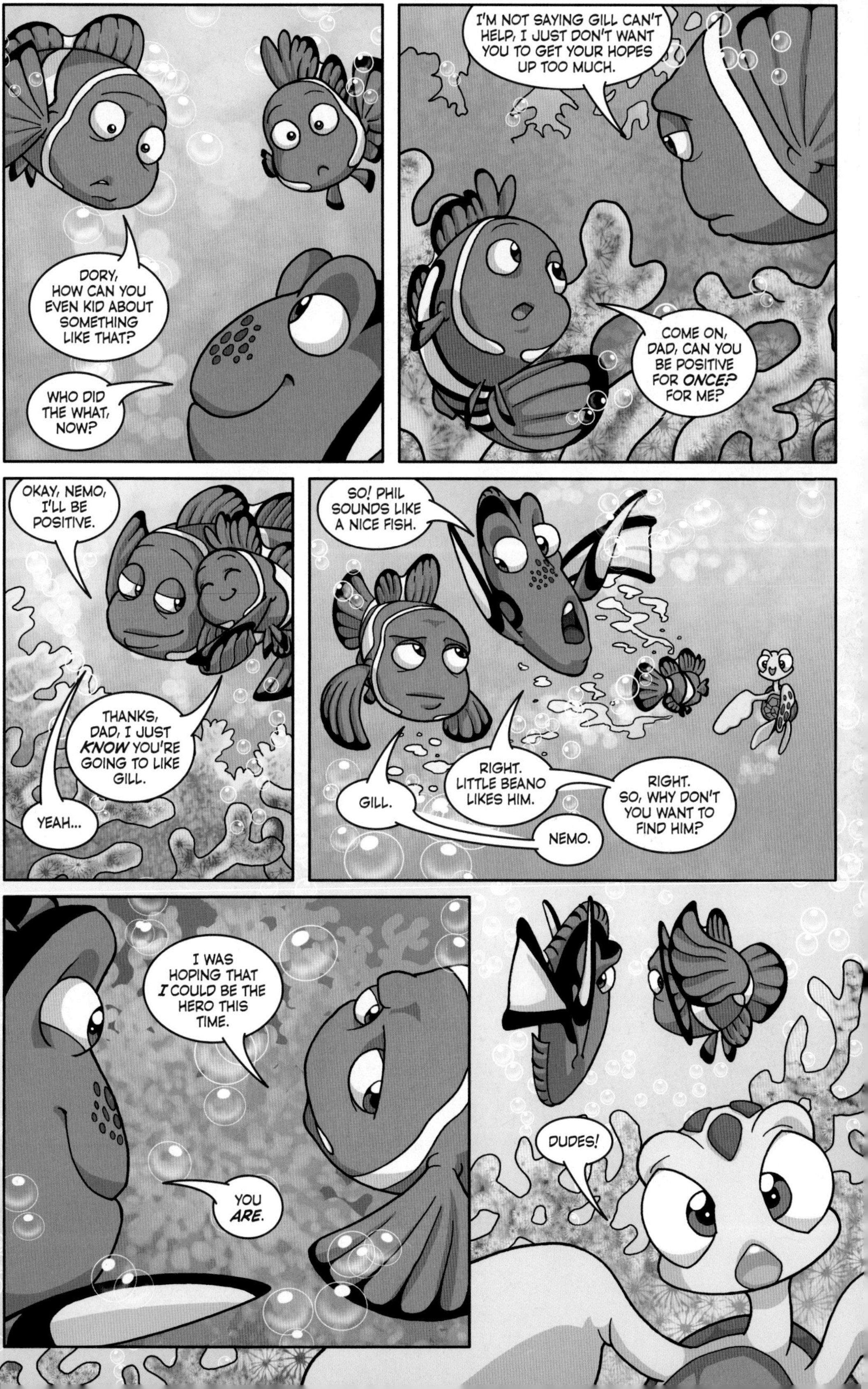
DORY, HOW CAN YOU EVEN KID ABOUT SOMETHING LIKE THAT?
WHO DID THE WHAT, NOW?
I'M NOT SAYING GILL CAN'T HELP, I JUST DON'T WANT YOU TO GET YOUR HOPES UP TOO MUCH.
COME ON, DAD, CAN YOU BE POSITIVE FOR *ONCE?* FOR ME?
OKAY, NEMO, I'LL BE POSITIVE.
THANKS, DAD, I JUST *KNOW* YOU'RE GOING TO LIKE GILL.
YEAH...
SO! PHIL SOUNDS LIKE A NICE FISH.
GILL.
RIGHT. LITTLE BEANO LIKES HIM.
NEMO.
RIGHT. SO, WHY DON'T YOU WANT TO FIND HIM?
I WAS HOPING THAT *I* COULD BE THE HERO THIS TIME.
YOU *ARE*.
DUDES!

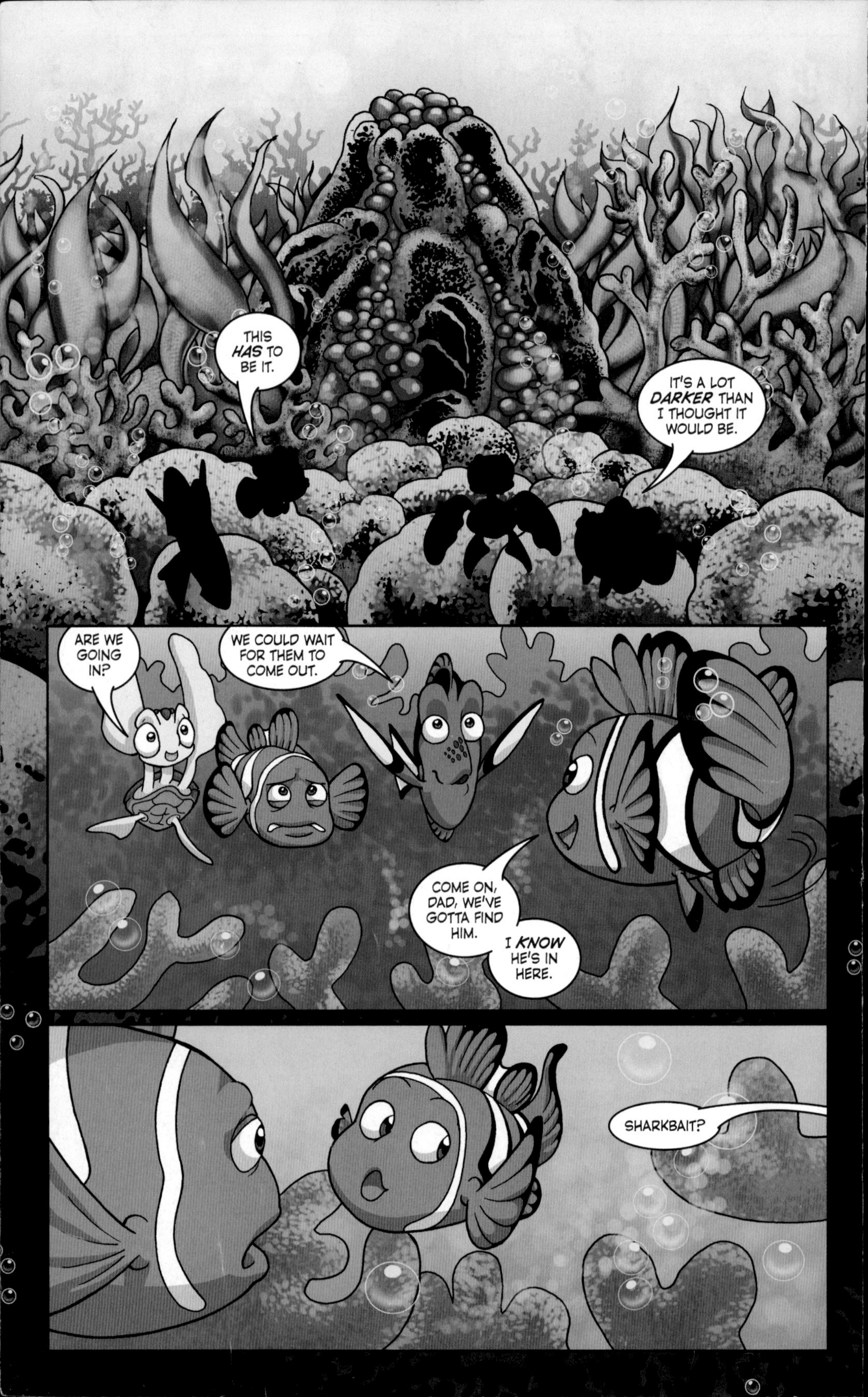
THIS *HAS* TO BE IT.
IT'S A LOT *DARKER* THAN I THOUGHT IT WOULD BE.
ARE WE GOING IN?
WE COULD WAIT FOR THEM TO COME OUT.
COME ON, DAD, WE'VE GOTTA FIND HIM.
I *KNOW* HE'S IN HERE.
SHARKBAIT?

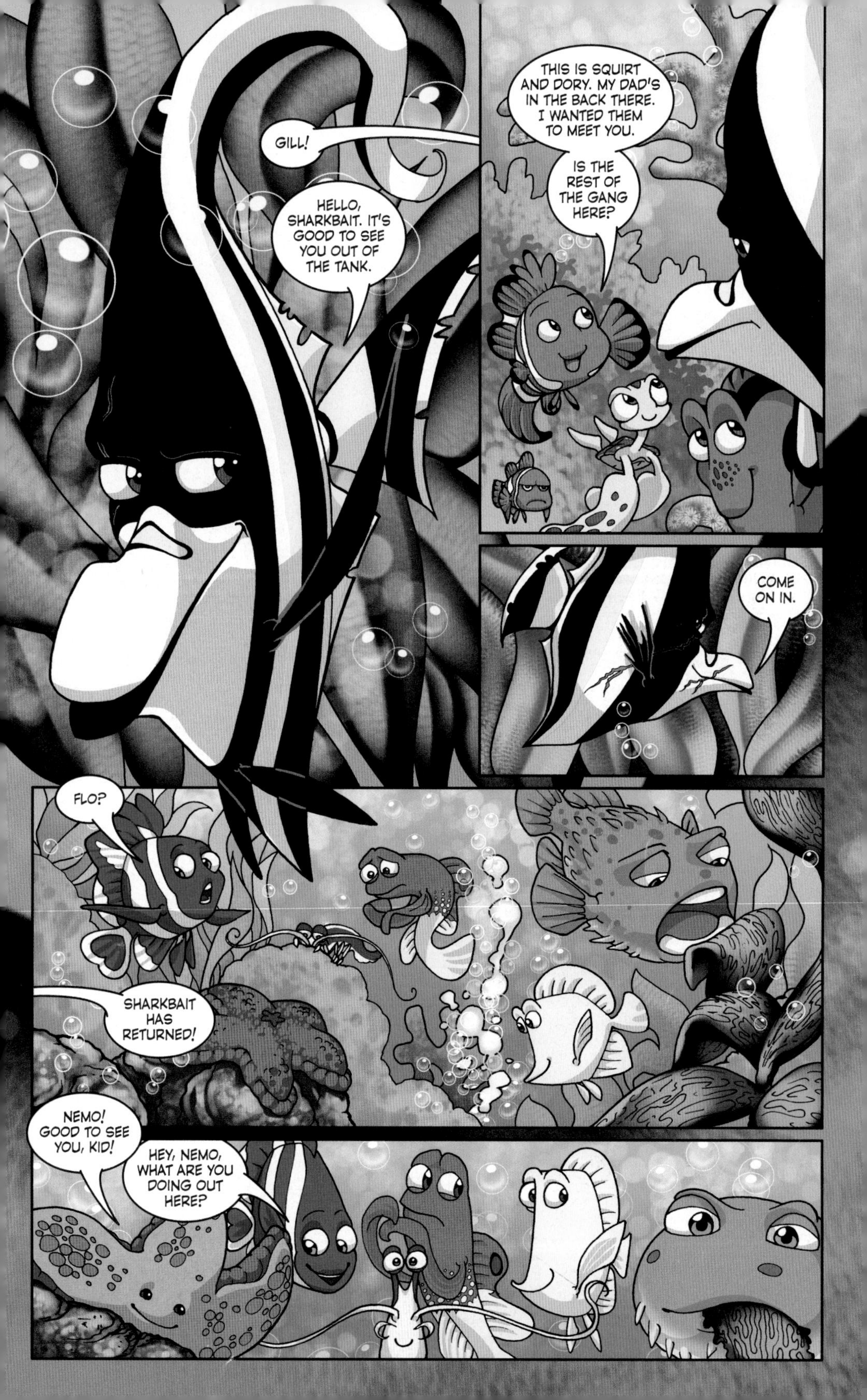
GILL!
HELLO, SHARKBAIT. IT'S GOOD TO SEE YOU OUT OF THE TANK.
THIS IS SQUIRT AND DORY. MY DAD'S IN THE BACK THERE. I WANTED THEM TO MEET YOU.
IS THE REST OF THE GANG HERE?
COME ON IN.
FLO?
SHARKBAIT HAS RETURNED!
NEMO! GOOD TO SEE YOU, KID!
HEY, NEMO, WHAT ARE YOU DOING OUT HERE?

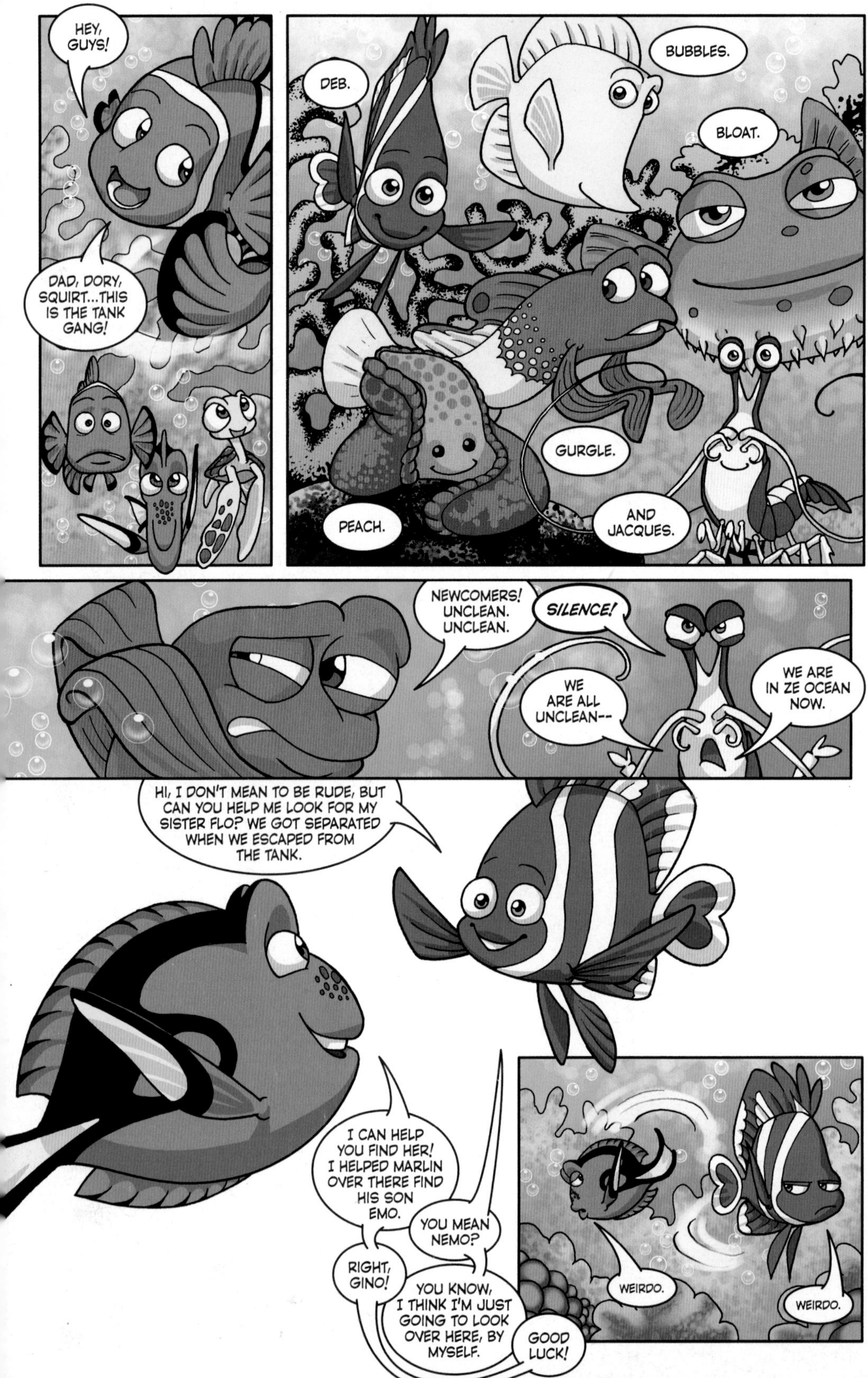
HEY, GUYS!
DAD, DORY, SQUIRT...THIS IS THE TANK GANG!
DEB.
BUBBLES.
BLOAT.
GURGLE.
PEACH.
AND JACQUES.
NEWCOMERS! UNCLEAN. UNCLEAN.
SILENCE!
WE ARE ALL UNCLEAN--
WE ARE IN ZE OCEAN NOW.
HI, I DON'T MEAN TO BE RUDE, BUT CAN YOU HELP ME LOOK FOR MY SISTER FLO? WE GOT SEPARATED WHEN WE ESCAPED FROM THE TANK.
I CAN HELP YOU FIND HER! I HELPED MARLIN OVER THERE FIND HIS SON EMO.
YOU MEAN NEMO?
RIGHT, GINO!
YOU KNOW, I THINK I'M JUST GOING TO LOOK OVER HERE, BY MYSELF.
GOOD LUCK!
WEIRDO.
WEIRDO.

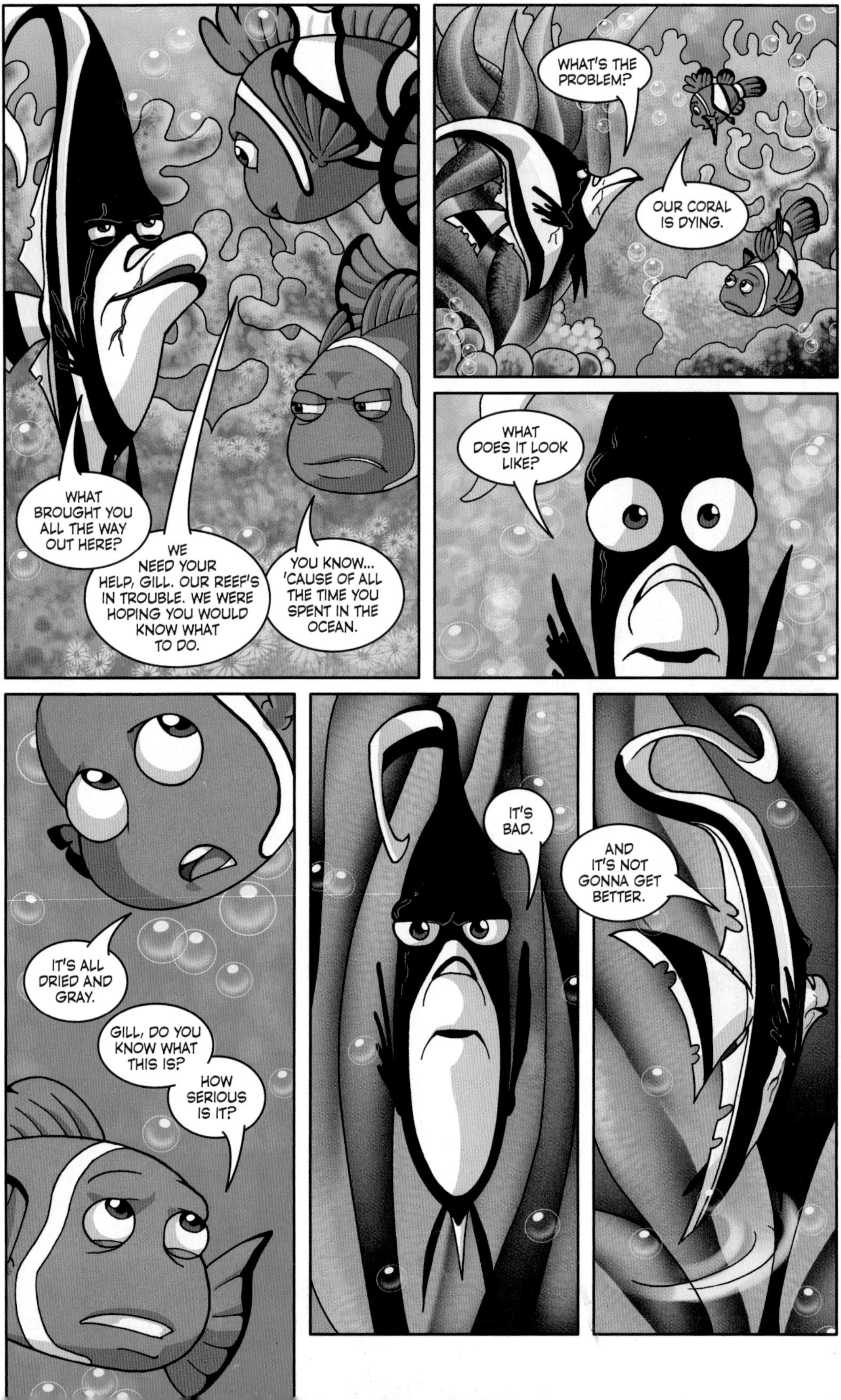
WHAT BROUGHT YOU ALL THE WAY OUT HERE?
WE NEED YOUR HELP, GILL. OUR REEF'S IN TROUBLE. WE WERE HOPING YOU WOULD KNOW WHAT TO DO.
YOU KNOW... 'CAUSE OF ALL THE TIME YOU SPENT IN THE OCEAN.
WHAT'S THE PROBLEM?
OUR CORAL IS DYING.
WHAT DOES IT LOOK LIKE?
IT'S ALL DRIED AND GRAY.
GILL, DO YOU KNOW WHAT THIS IS?
HOW SERIOUS IS IT?
IT'S BAD.
AND IT'S NOT GONNA GET BETTER.

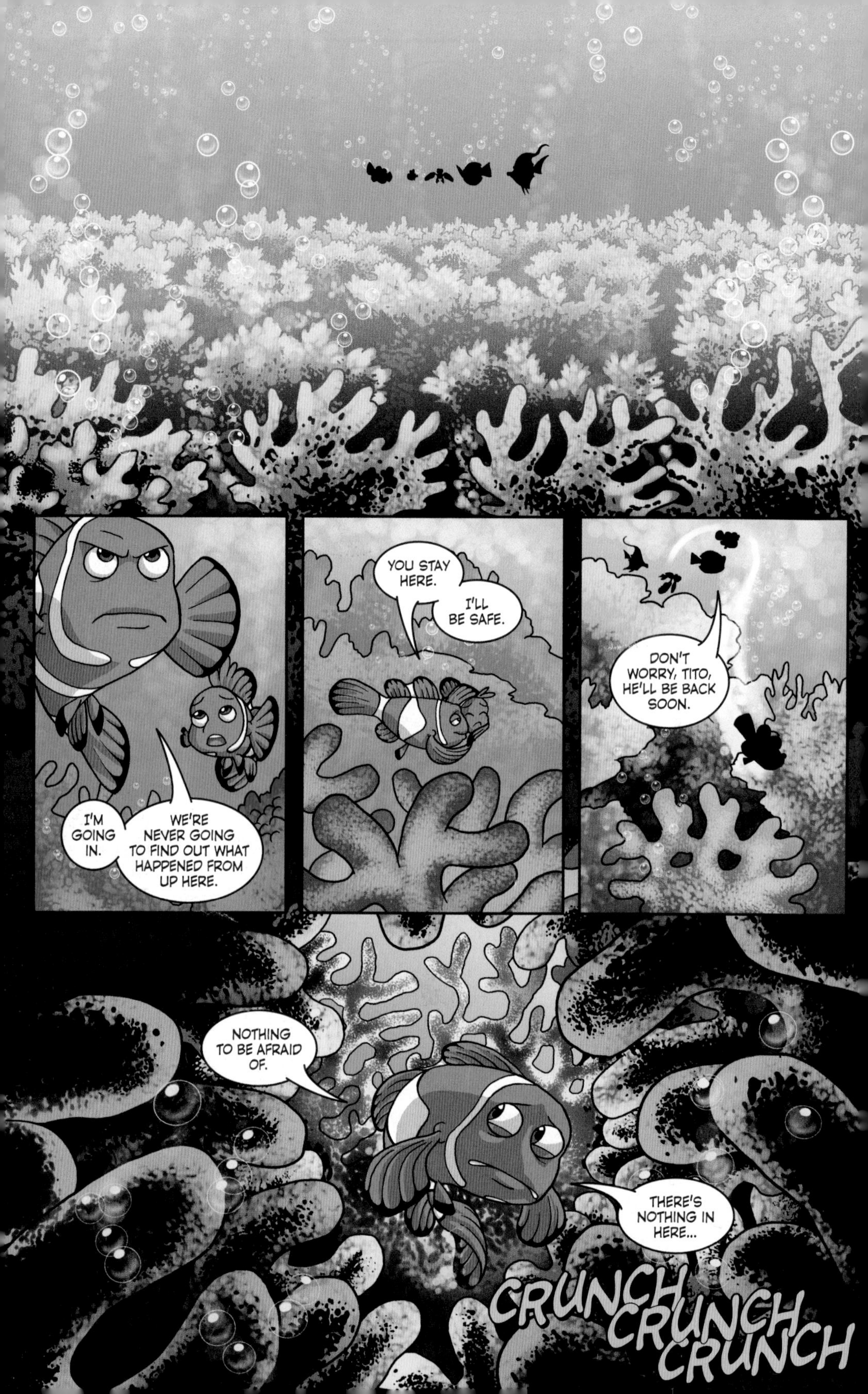
I'M GOING IN.
WE'RE NEVER GOING TO FIND OUT WHAT HAPPENED FROM UP HERE.
YOU STAY HERE.
I'LL BE SAFE.
DON'T WORRY, TITO, HE'LL BE BACK SOON.
NOTHING TO BE AFRAID OF.
THERE'S NOTHING IN HERE...
CRUNCH CRUNCH CRUNCH

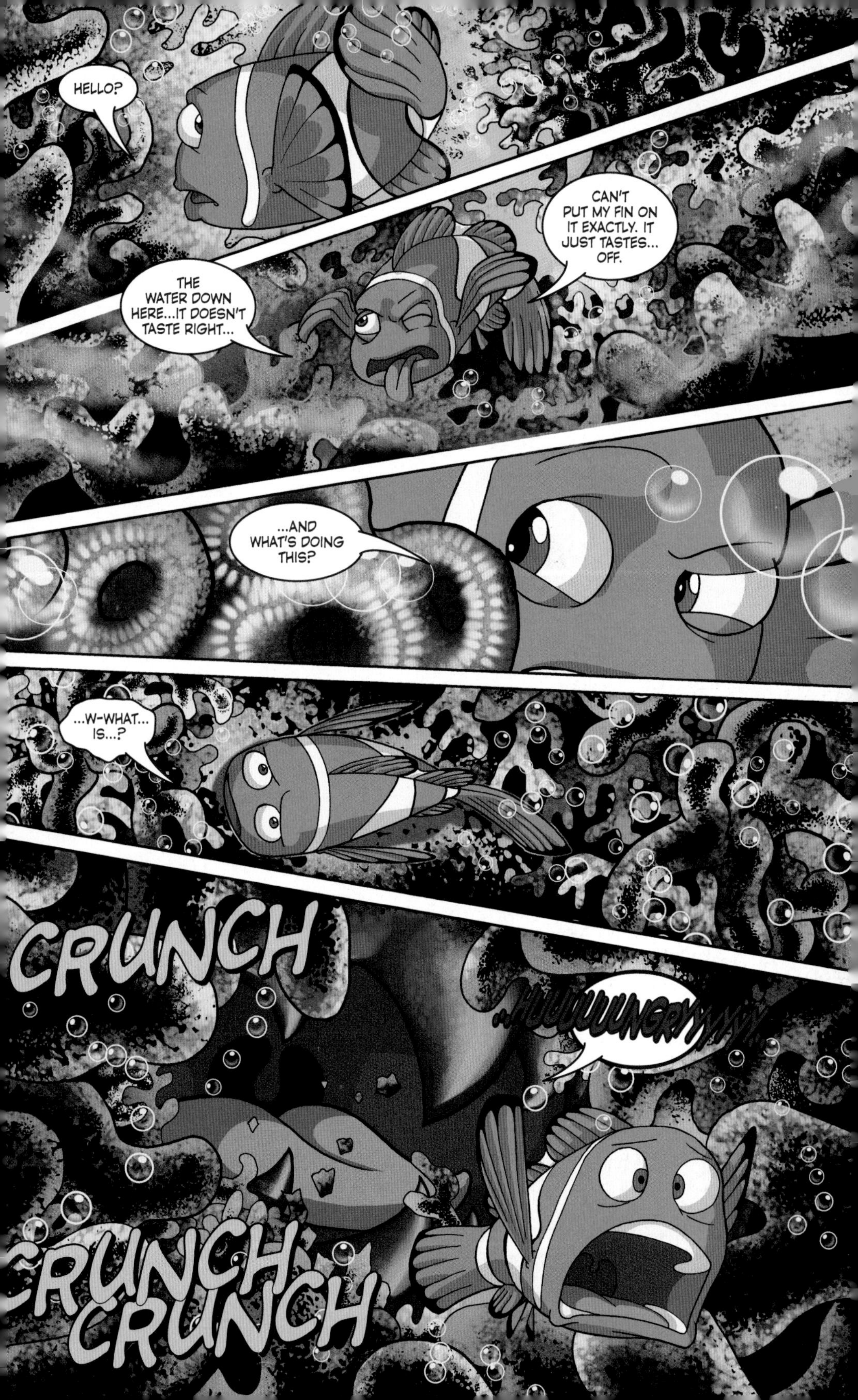
HELLO?
THE WATER DOWN HERE...IT DOESN'T TASTE RIGHT...
CAN'T PUT MY FIN ON IT EXACTLY. IT JUST TASTES... OFF.
...AND WHAT'S DOING THIS?
...W-WHAT... IS...?
CRUNCH
..HUUUUUNGRYYYYY
CRUNCH
CRUNCH

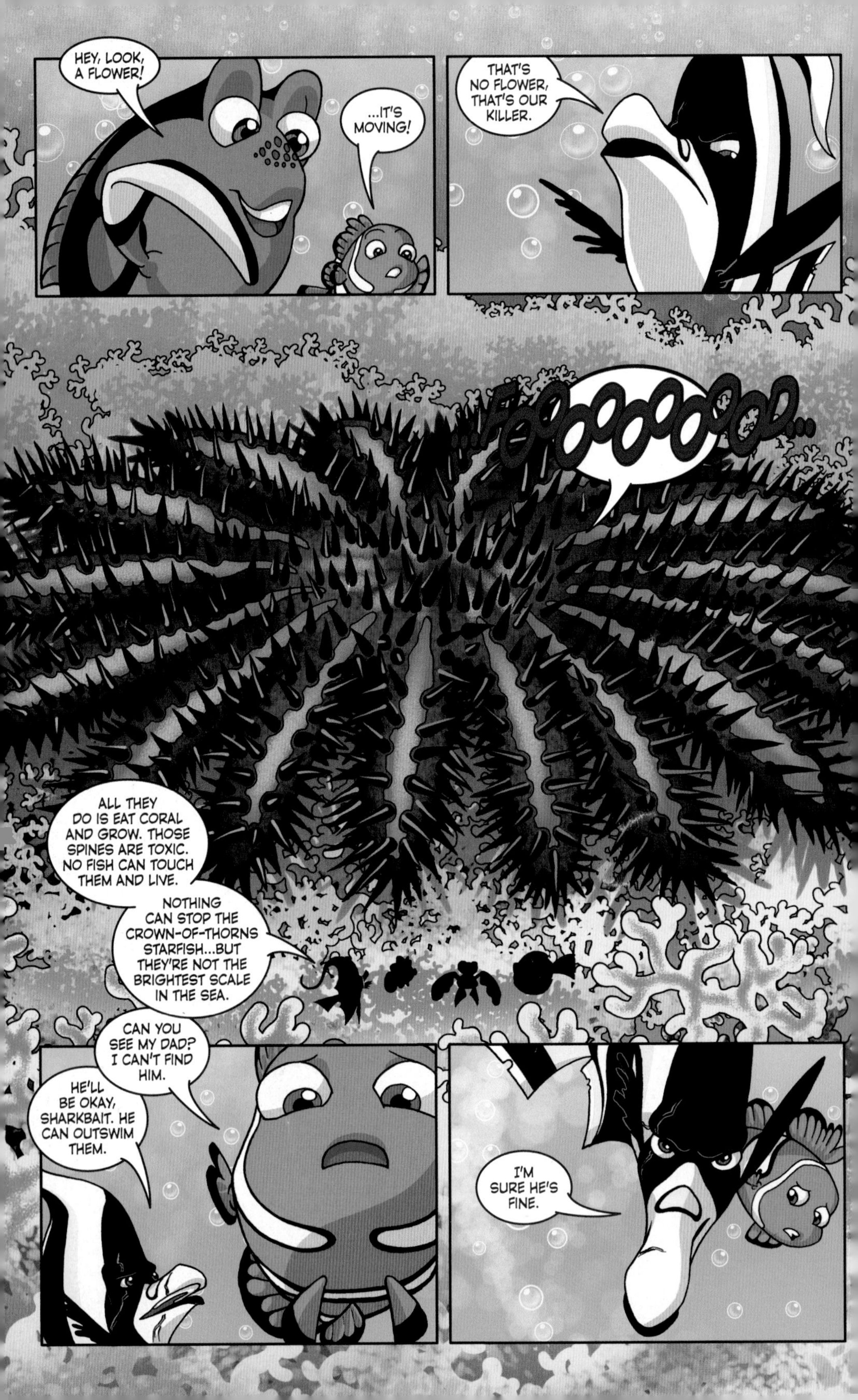
HEY, LOOK, A FLOWER!
...IT'S MOVING!
THAT'S NO FLOWER, THAT'S OUR KILLER.
...FOOOOOOOOOD...
ALL THEY DO IS EAT CORAL AND GROW. THOSE SPINES ARE TOXIC. NO FISH CAN TOUCH THEM AND LIVE.
NOTHING CAN STOP THE CROWN-OF-THORNS STARFISH...BUT THEY'RE NOT THE BRIGHTEST SCALE IN THE SEA.
CAN YOU SEE MY DAD? I CAN'T FIND HIM.
HE'LL BE OKAY, SHARKBAIT. HE CAN OUTSWIM THEM.
I'M SURE HE'S FINE.

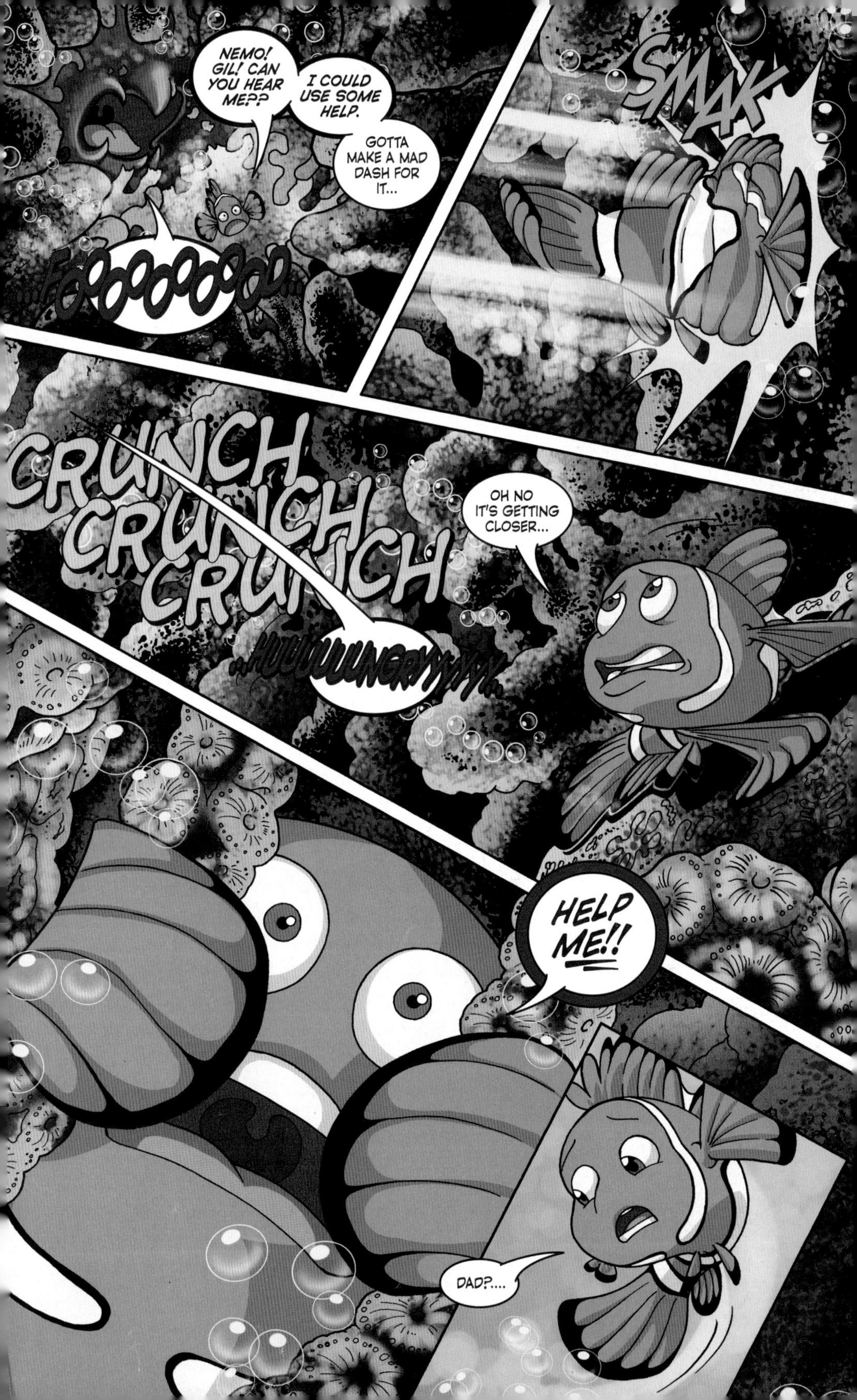
NEMO! GIL! CAN YOU HEAR ME??
I COULD USE SOME HELP.
GOTTA MAKE A MAD DASH FOR IT...
...FOOOOOOOOOD...
SMAK
CRUNCH
CRUNCH
CRUNCH
...HUUUUUNGRYYYYY...
OH NO IT'S GETTING CLOSER...
HELP ME!!
DAD?....

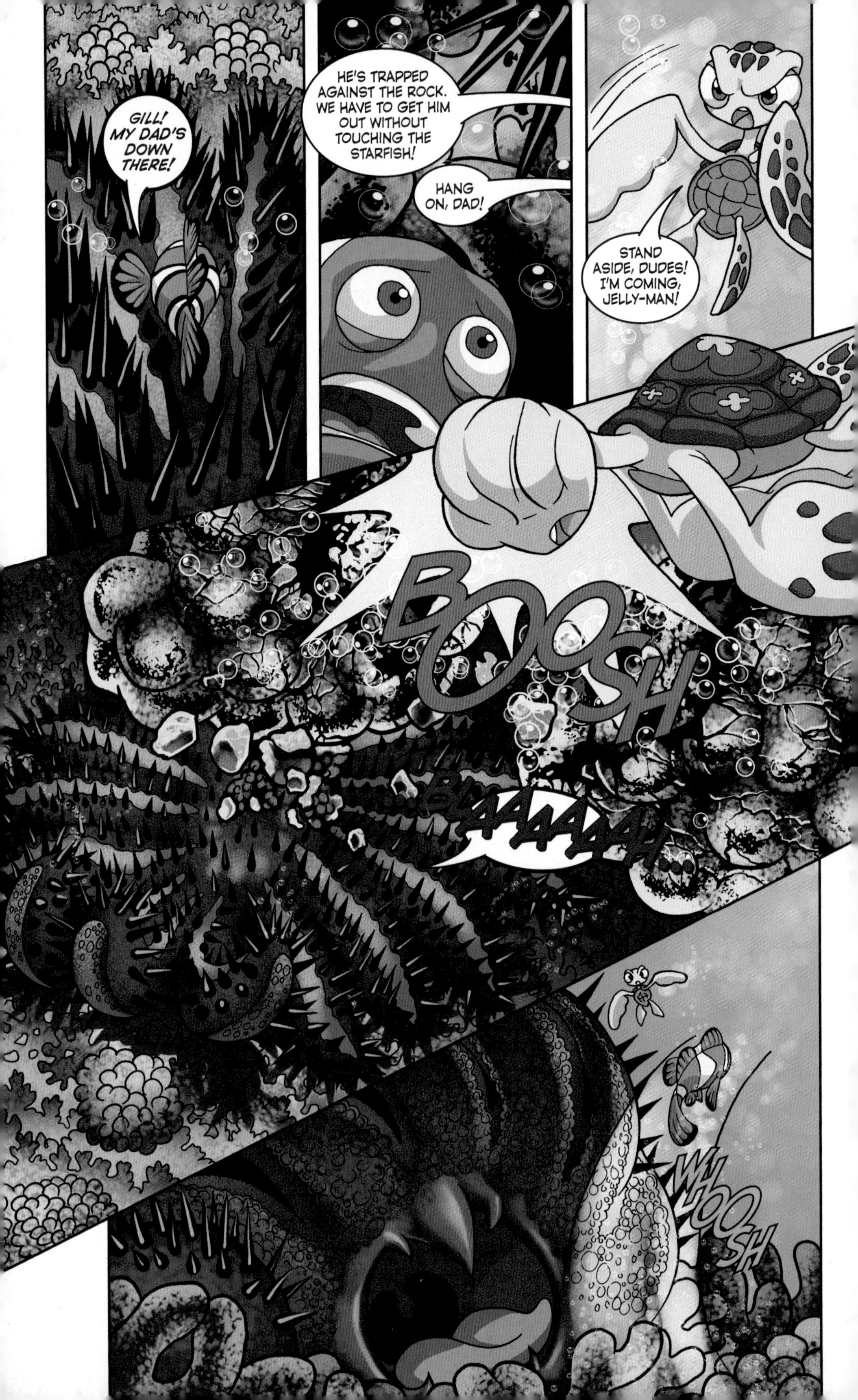

GILL! MY DAD'S DOWN THERE!
HE'S TRAPPED AGAINST THE ROCK. WE HAVE TO GET HIM OUT WITHOUT TOUCHING THE STARFISH!
HANG ON, DAD!
STAND ASIDE, DUDES! I'M COMING, JELLY-MAN!
BOOSH
BLAAAAAAH!
WHOOSH

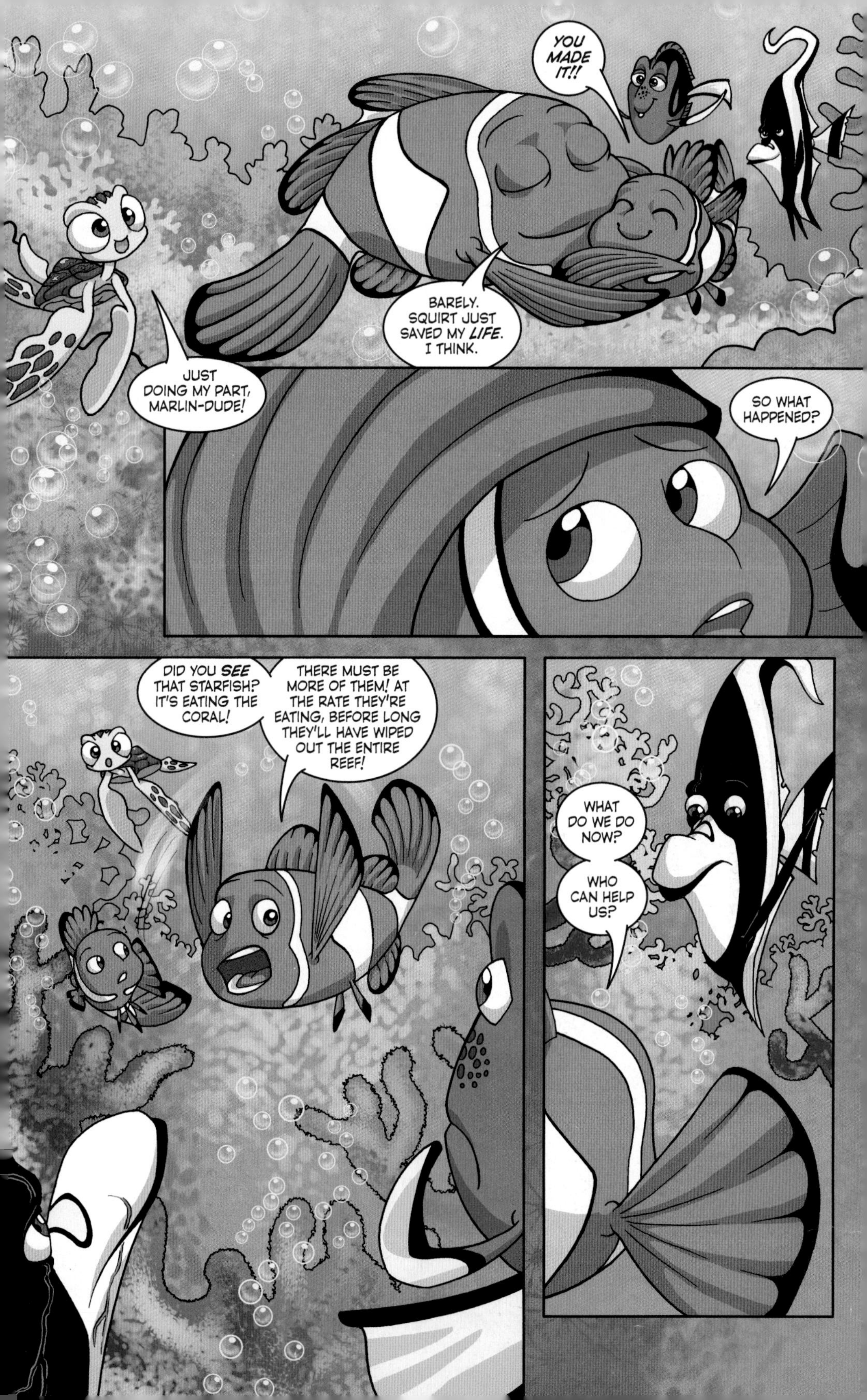
YOU MADE IT!!
BARELY. SQUIRT JUST SAVED MY LIFE. I THINK.
JUST DOING MY PART, MARLIN-DUDE!
SO WHAT HAPPENED?
DID YOU SEE THAT STARFISH? IT'S EATING THE CORAL!
THERE MUST BE MORE OF THEM! AT THE RATE THEY'RE EATING, BEFORE LONG THEY'LL HAVE WIPED OUT THE ENTIRE REEF!
WHAT DO WE DO NOW?
WHO CAN HELP US?

# CHAPTER THREE

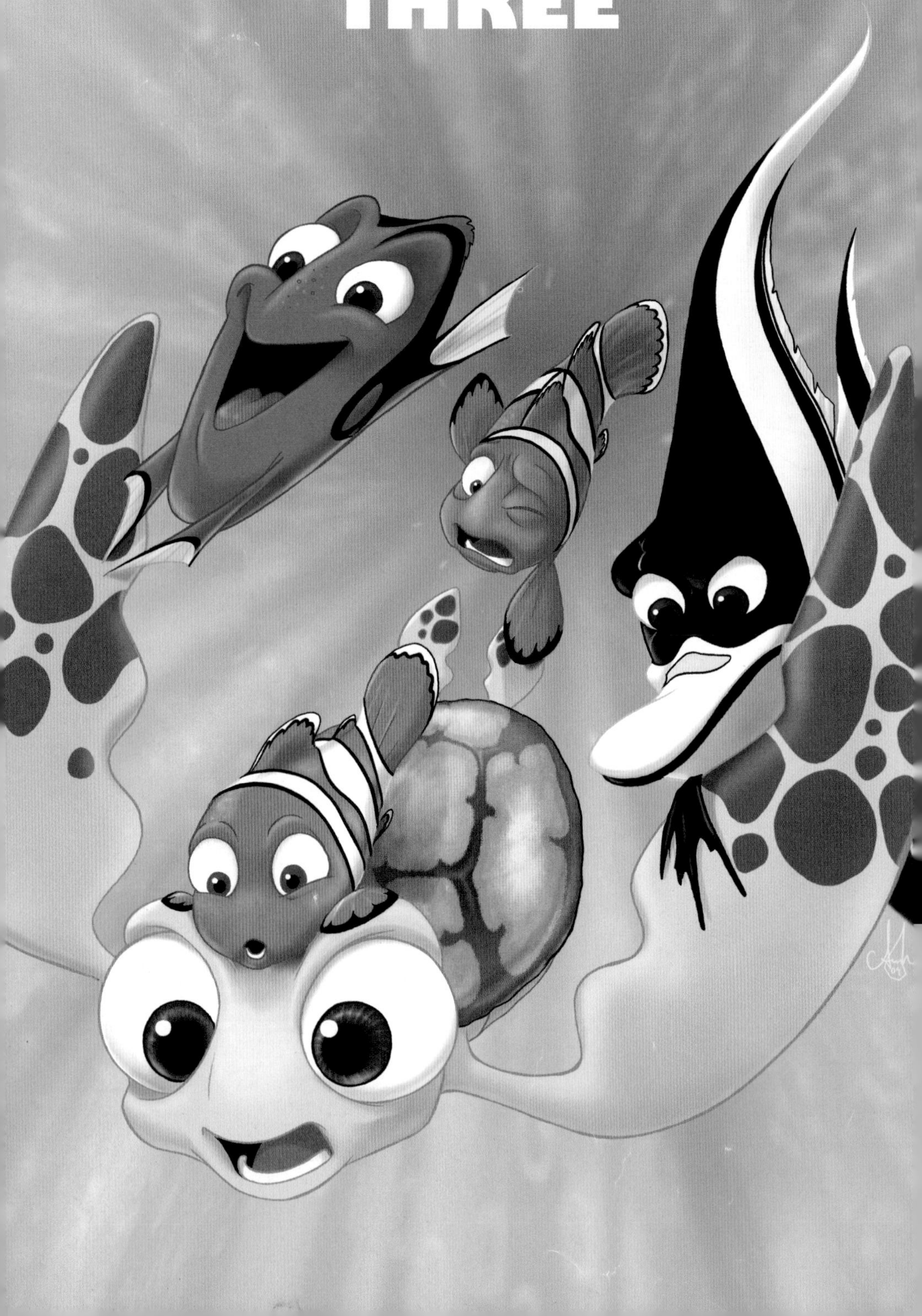

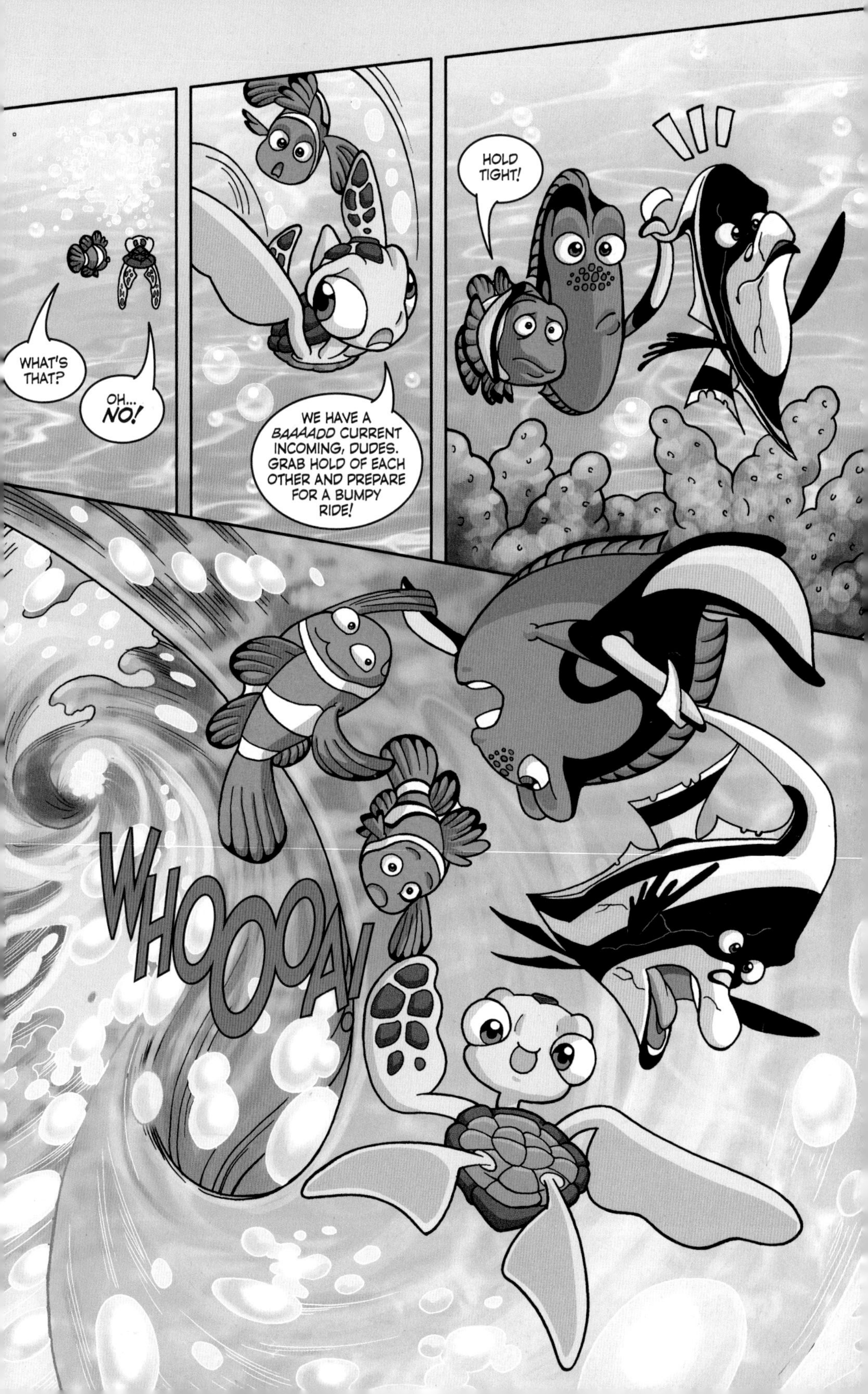
WHAT'S THAT?
OH... NO!
WE HAVE A BAAAADD CURRENT INCOMING, DUDES. GRAB HOLD OF EACH OTHER AND PREPARE FOR A BUMPY RIDE!
HOLD TIGHT!
WHOOOA!

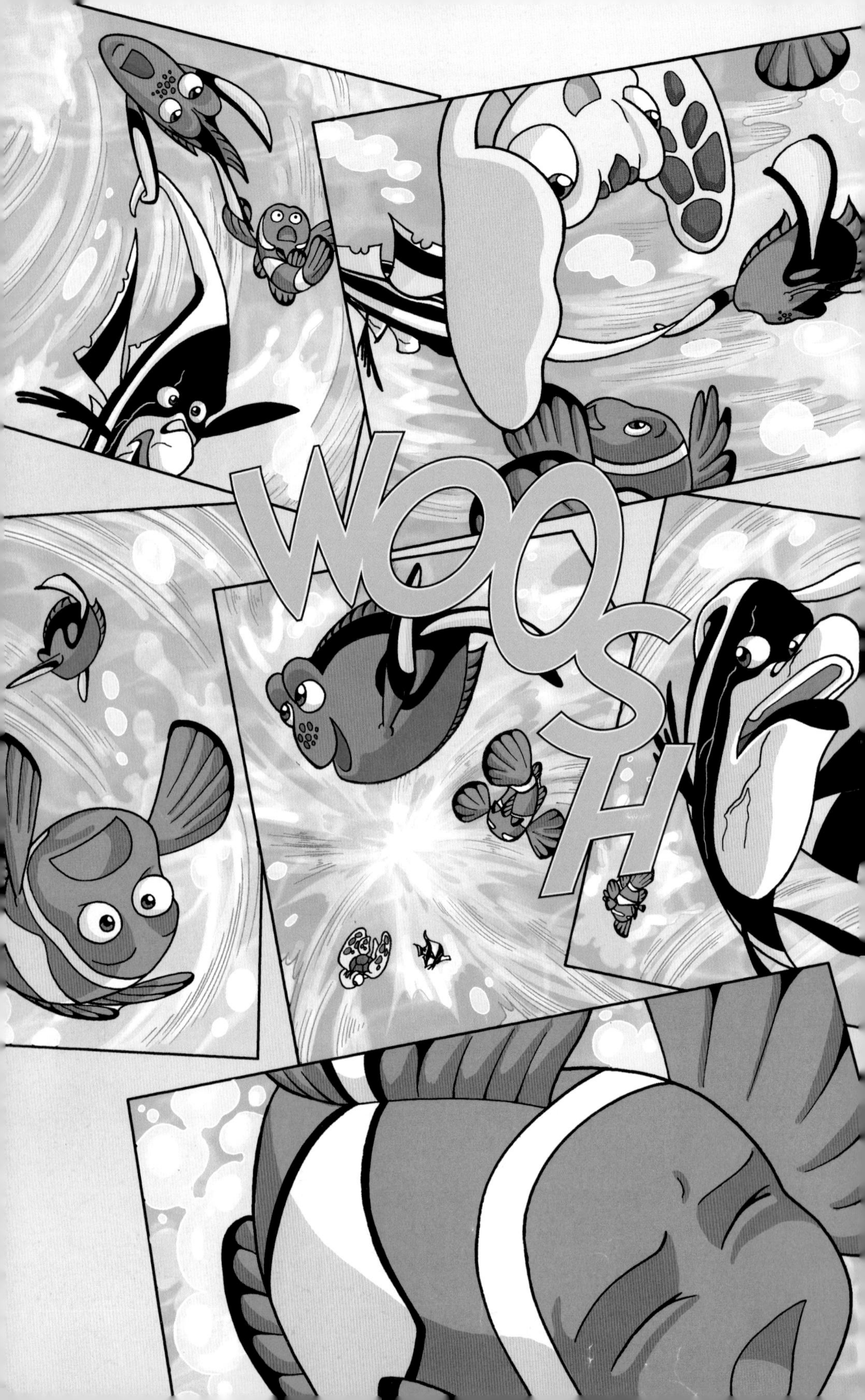
WOOSH

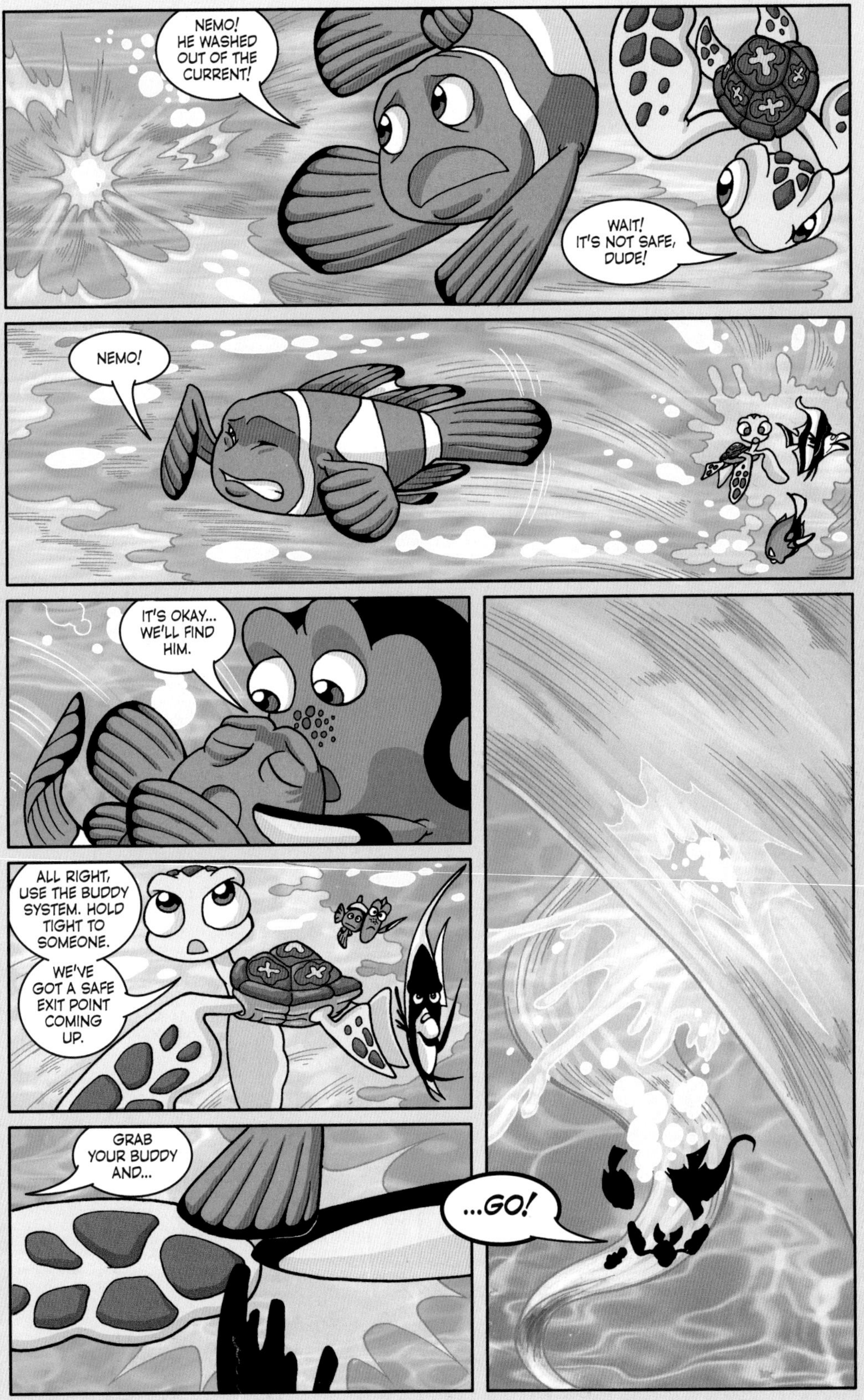
NEMO! HE WASHED OUT OF THE CURRENT!
WAIT! IT'S NOT SAFE, DUDE!
NEMO!
IT'S OKAY... WE'LL FIND HIM.
ALL RIGHT, USE THE BUDDY SYSTEM. HOLD TIGHT TO SOMEONE.
WE'VE GOT A SAFE EXIT POINT COMING UP.
GRAB YOUR BUDDY AND...
...GO!

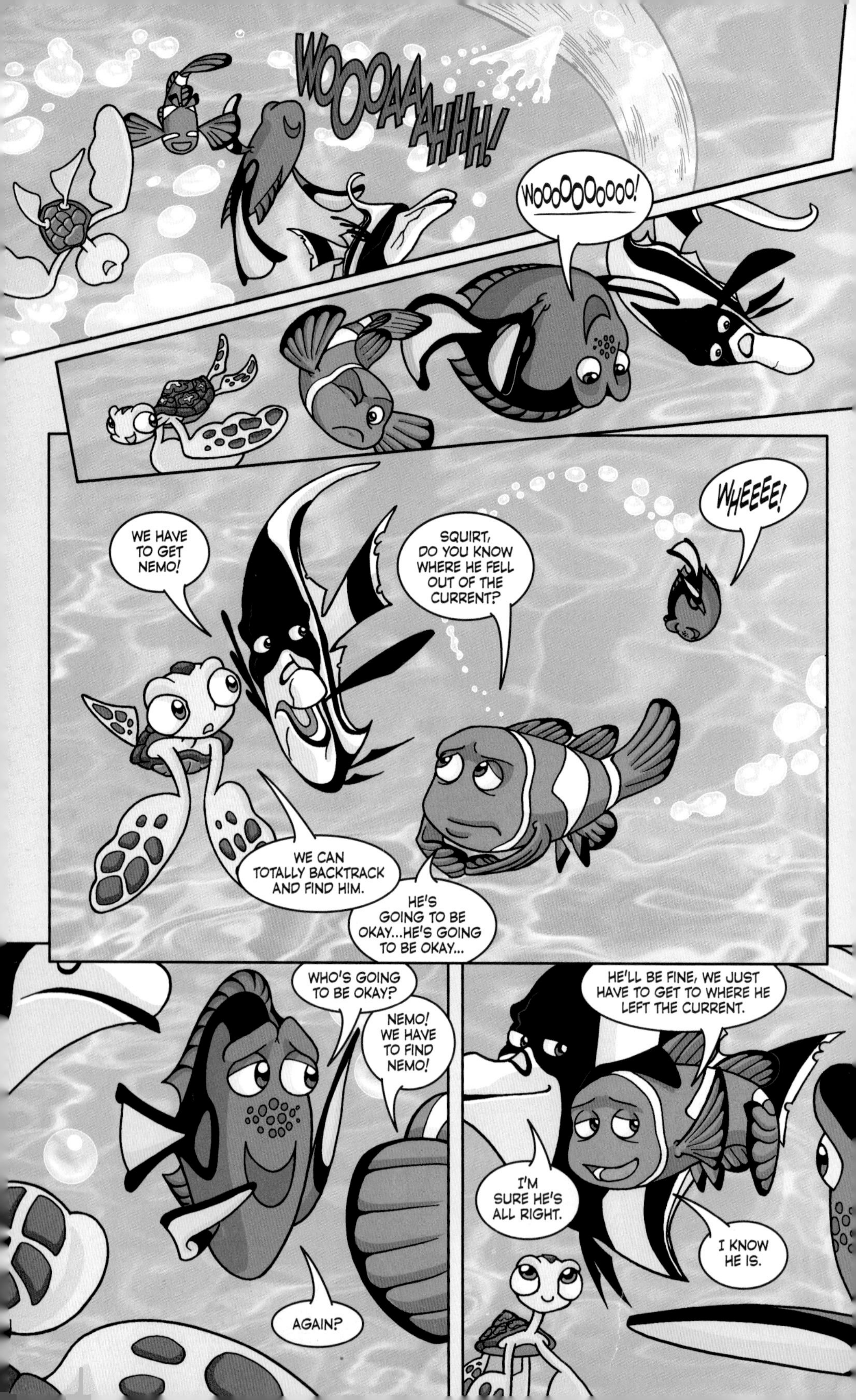
WOOOAAAAHHH!
WOOOOOOOOOO!
WHEEEE!
WE HAVE TO GET NEMO!
SQUIRT, DO YOU KNOW WHERE HE FELL OUT OF THE CURRENT?
WE CAN TOTALLY BACKTRACK AND FIND HIM.
HE'S GOING TO BE OKAY...HE'S GOING TO BE OKAY...
WHO'S GOING TO BE OKAY?
NEMO! WE HAVE TO FIND NEMO!
AGAIN?
HE'LL BE FINE, WE JUST HAVE TO GET TO WHERE HE LEFT THE CURRENT.
I'M SURE HE'S ALL RIGHT.
I KNOW HE IS.

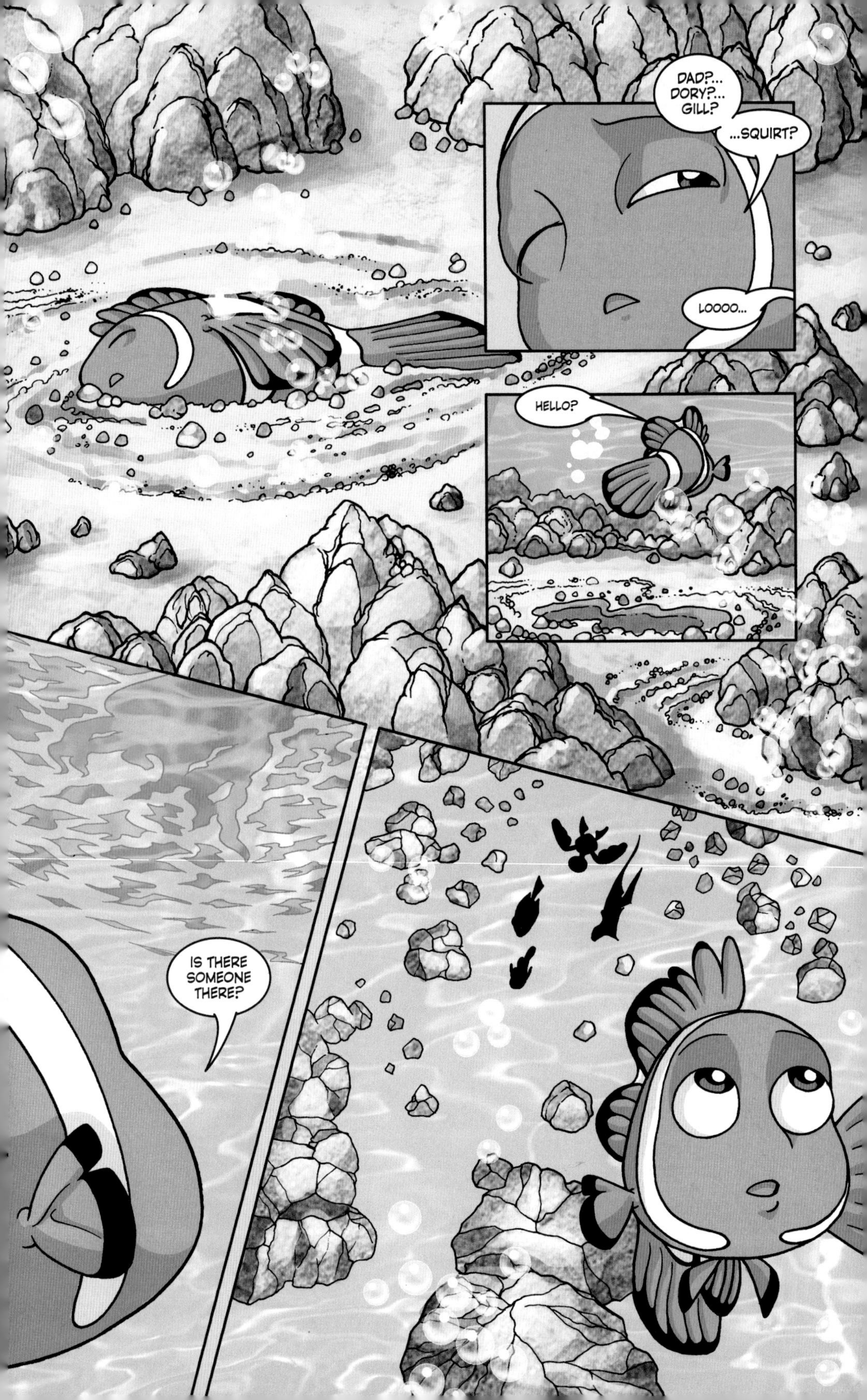
DAD?...
DORY?...
GILL?
...SQUIRT?
LOOOO...
HELLO?
IS THERE SOMEONE THERE?

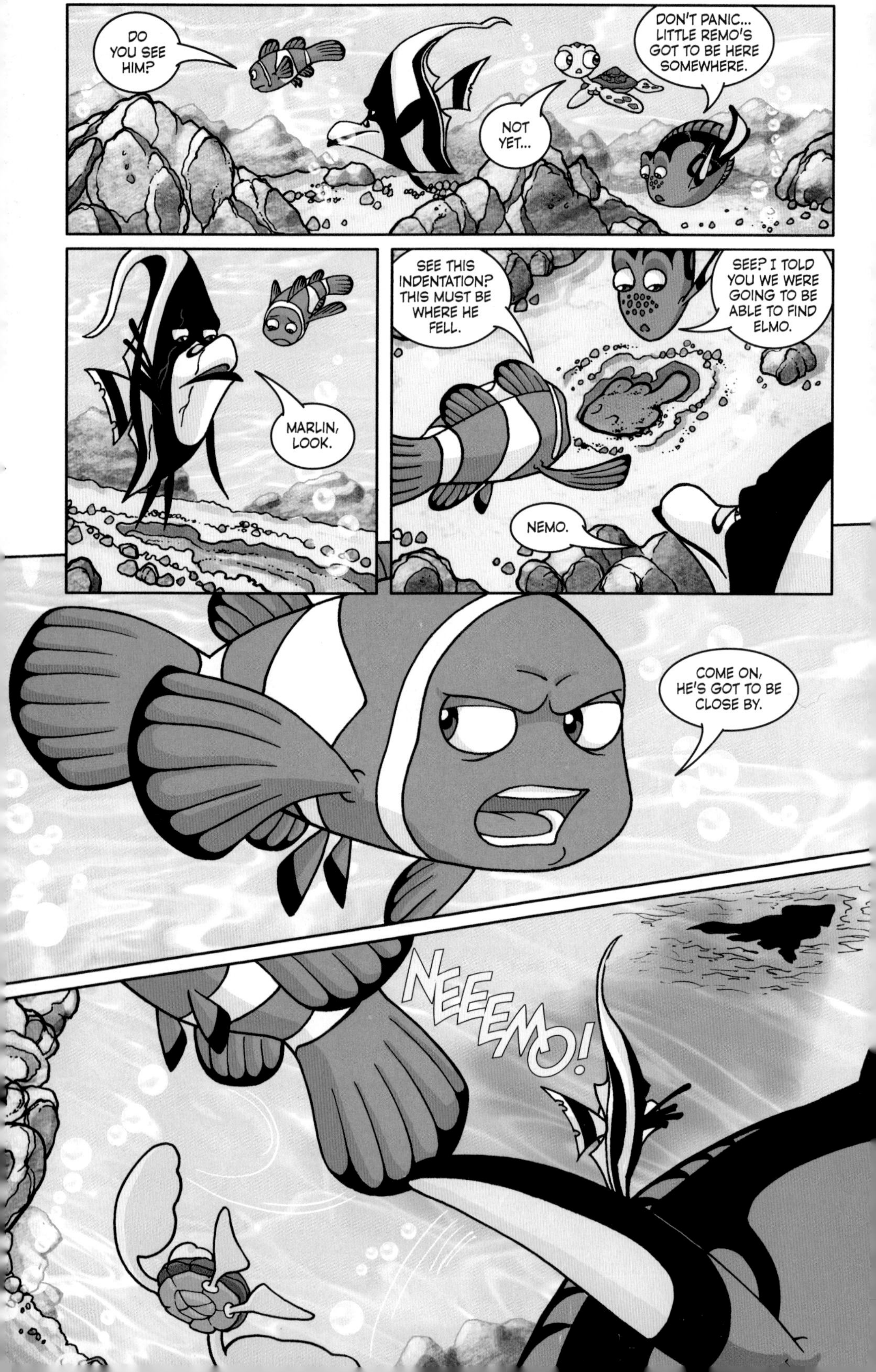
DO YOU SEE HIM?
DON'T PANIC... LITTLE REMO'S GOT TO BE HERE SOMEWHERE.
NOT YET...
MARLIN, LOOK.
SEE THIS INDENTATION? THIS MUST BE WHERE HE FELL.
SEE? I TOLD YOU WE WERE GOING TO BE ABLE TO FIND ELMO.
NEMO.
COME ON, HE'S GOT TO BE CLOSE BY.
NEEEEMO!

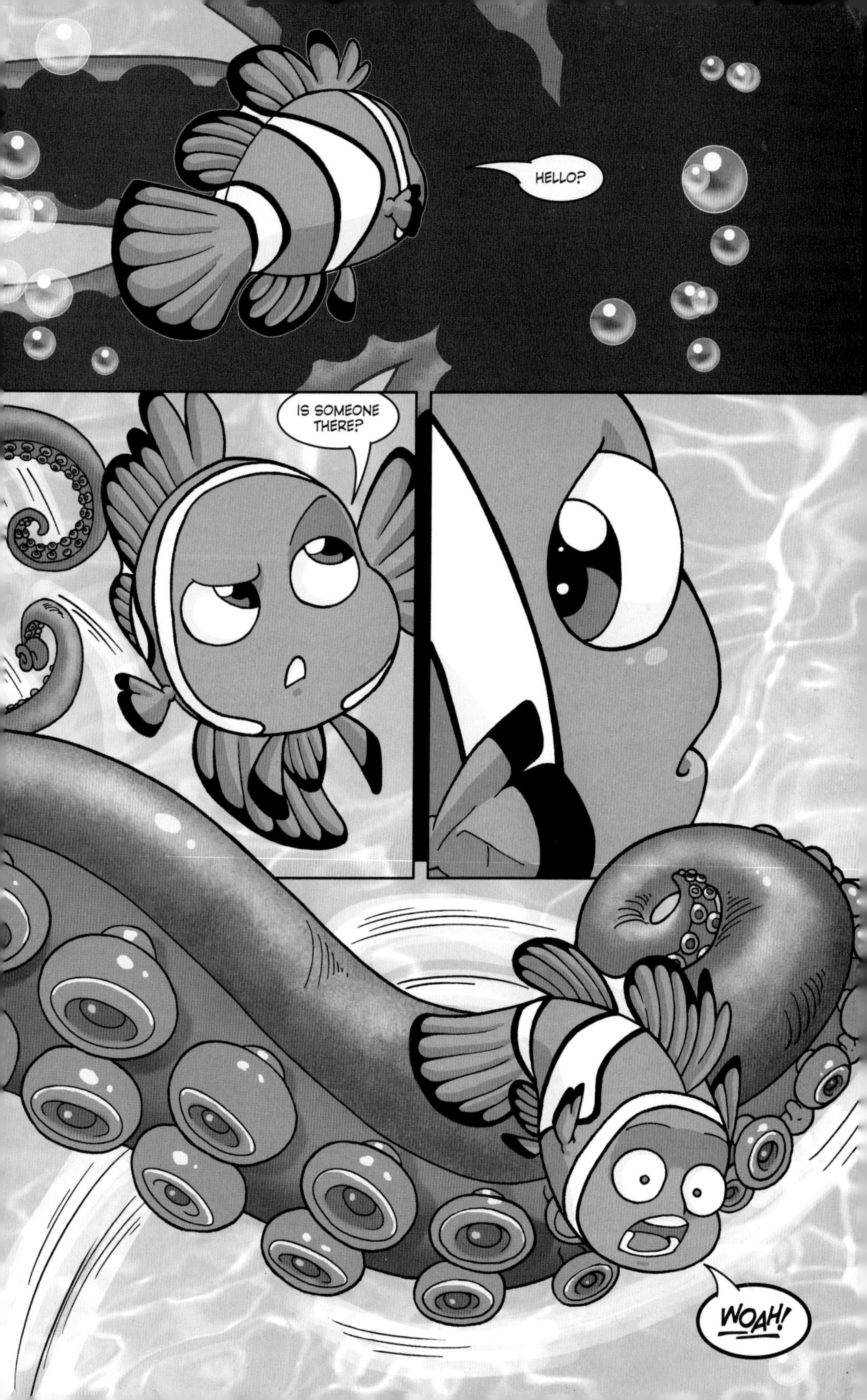
HELLO?
IS SOMEONE THERE?
WOAH!

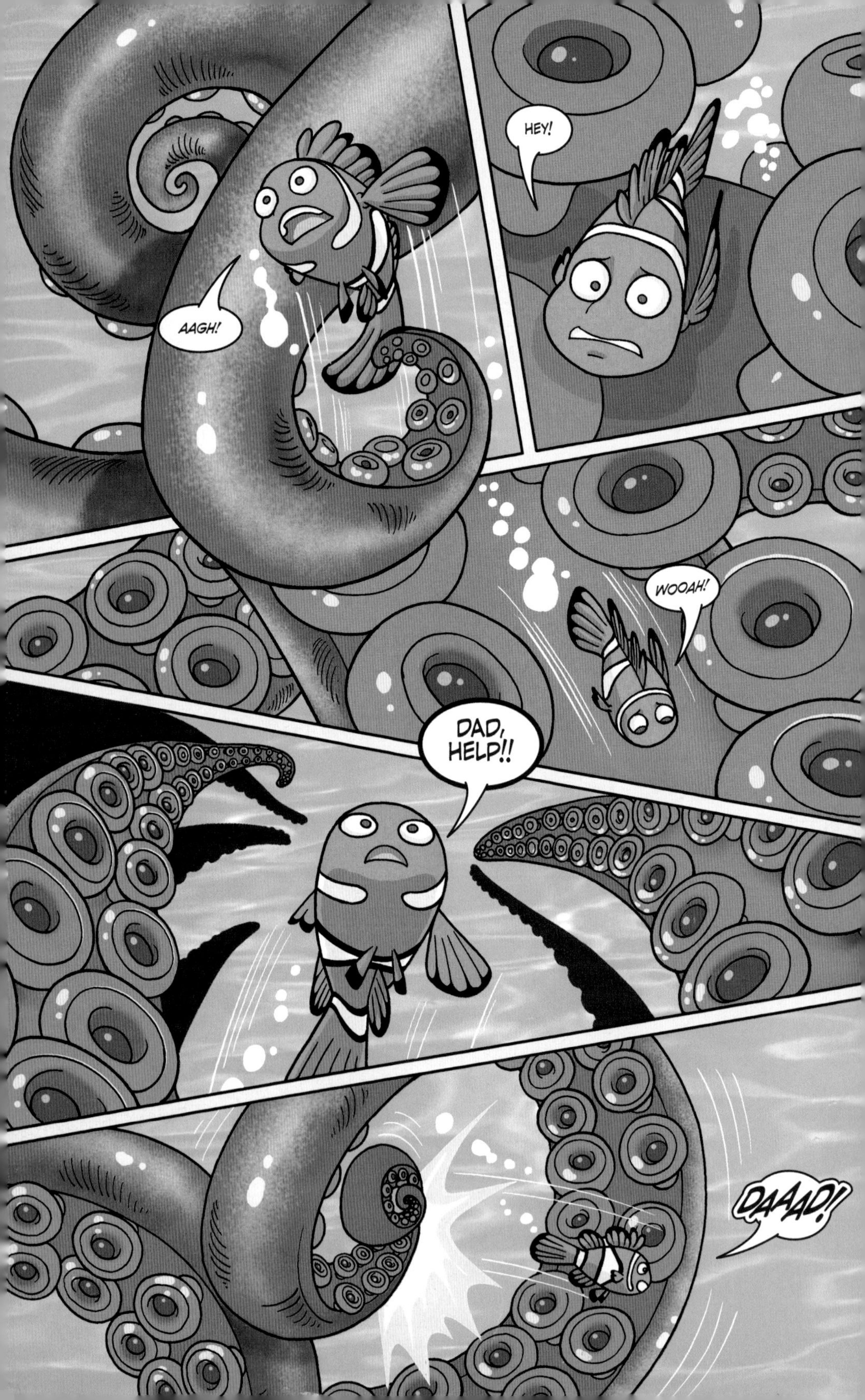
AAGH!
HEY!
WOOAH!
DAD, HELP!!
DAAAD!

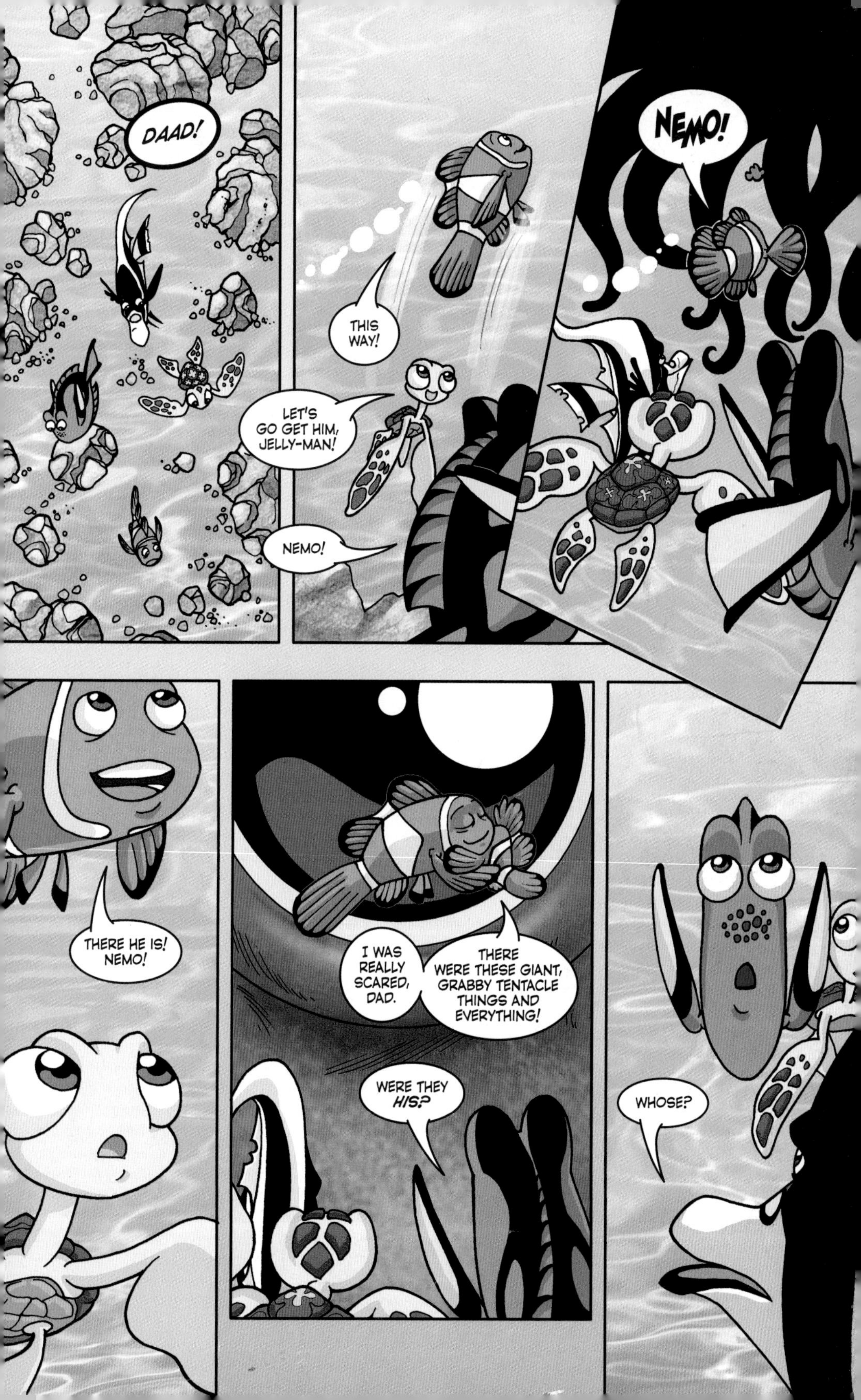
DAAD!
THIS WAY!
LET'S GO GET HIM, JELLY-MAN!
NEMO!
NEMO!
THERE HE IS! NEMO!
I WAS REALLY SCARED, DAD.
THERE WERE THESE GIANT, GRABBY TENTACLE THINGS AND EVERYTHING!
WERE THEY *HIS?*
WHOSE?

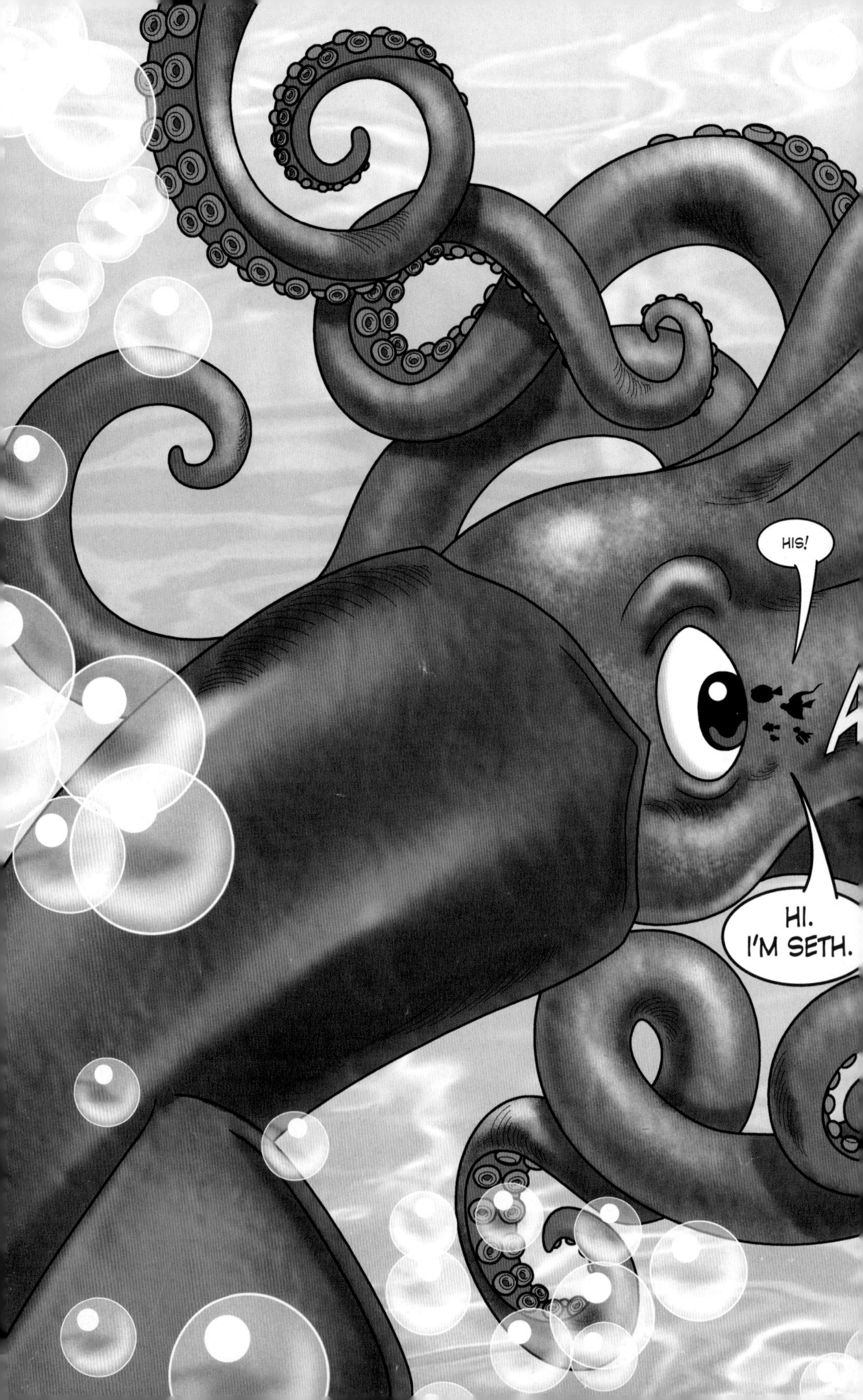
HIS!
HI. I'M SETH.

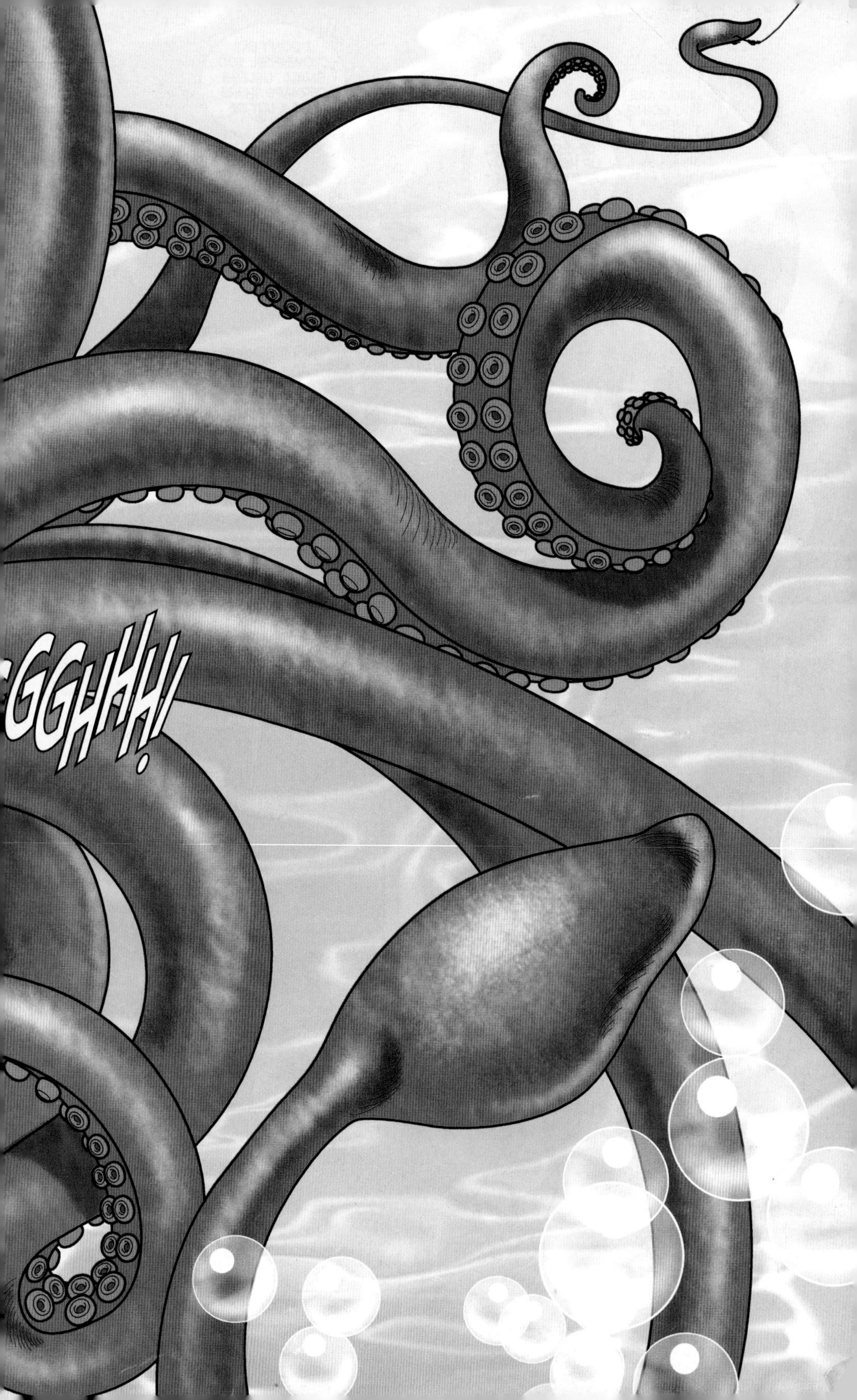
GGHHH!

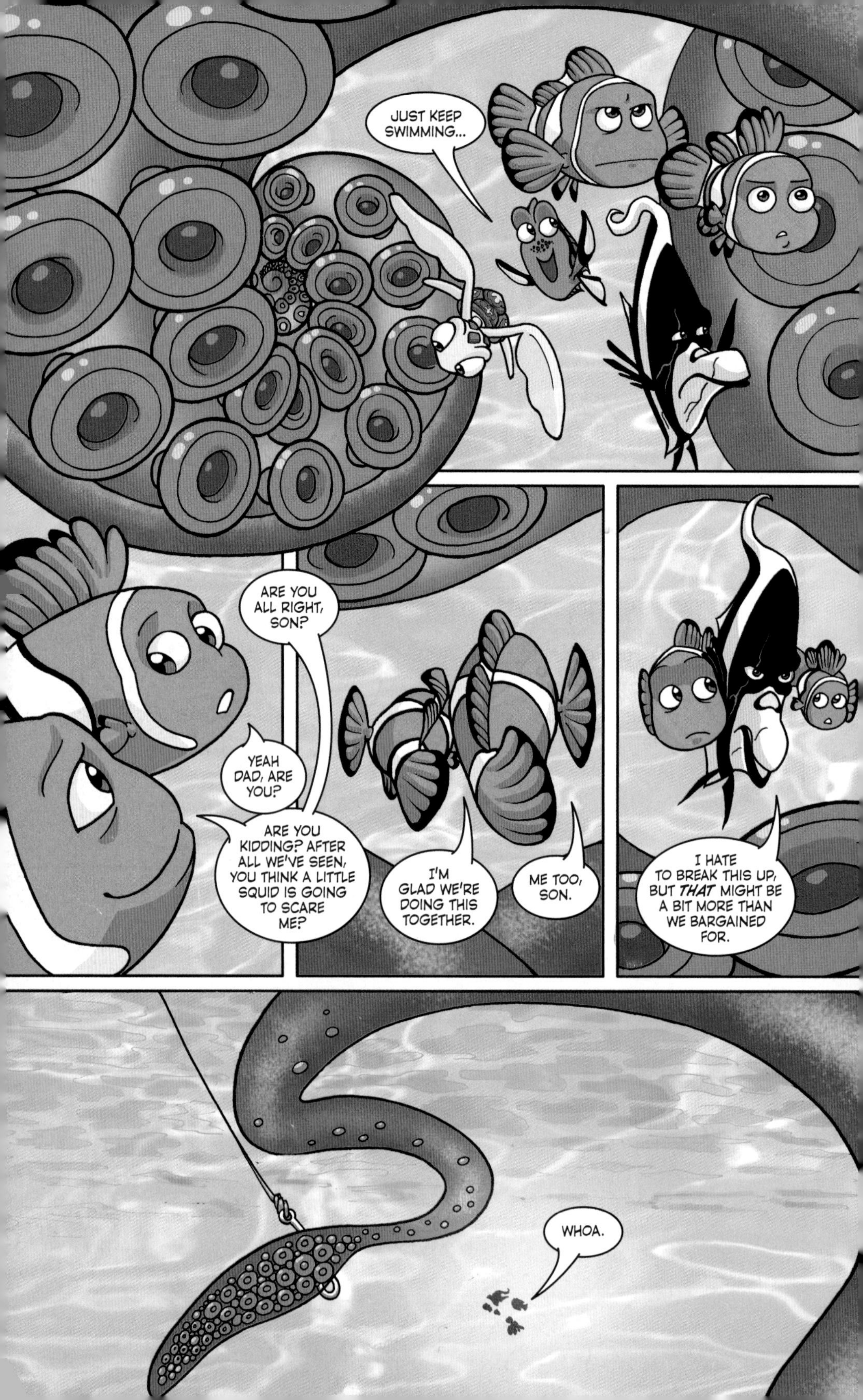
JUST KEEP SWIMMING...
ARE YOU ALL RIGHT, SON?
YEAH DAD, ARE YOU?
ARE YOU KIDDING? AFTER ALL WE'VE SEEN, YOU THINK A LITTLE SQUID IS GOING TO SCARE ME?
I'M GLAD WE'RE DOING THIS TOGETHER.
ME TOO, SON.
I HATE TO BREAK THIS UP, BUT *THAT* MIGHT BE A BIT MORE THAN WE BARGAINED FOR.
WHOA.

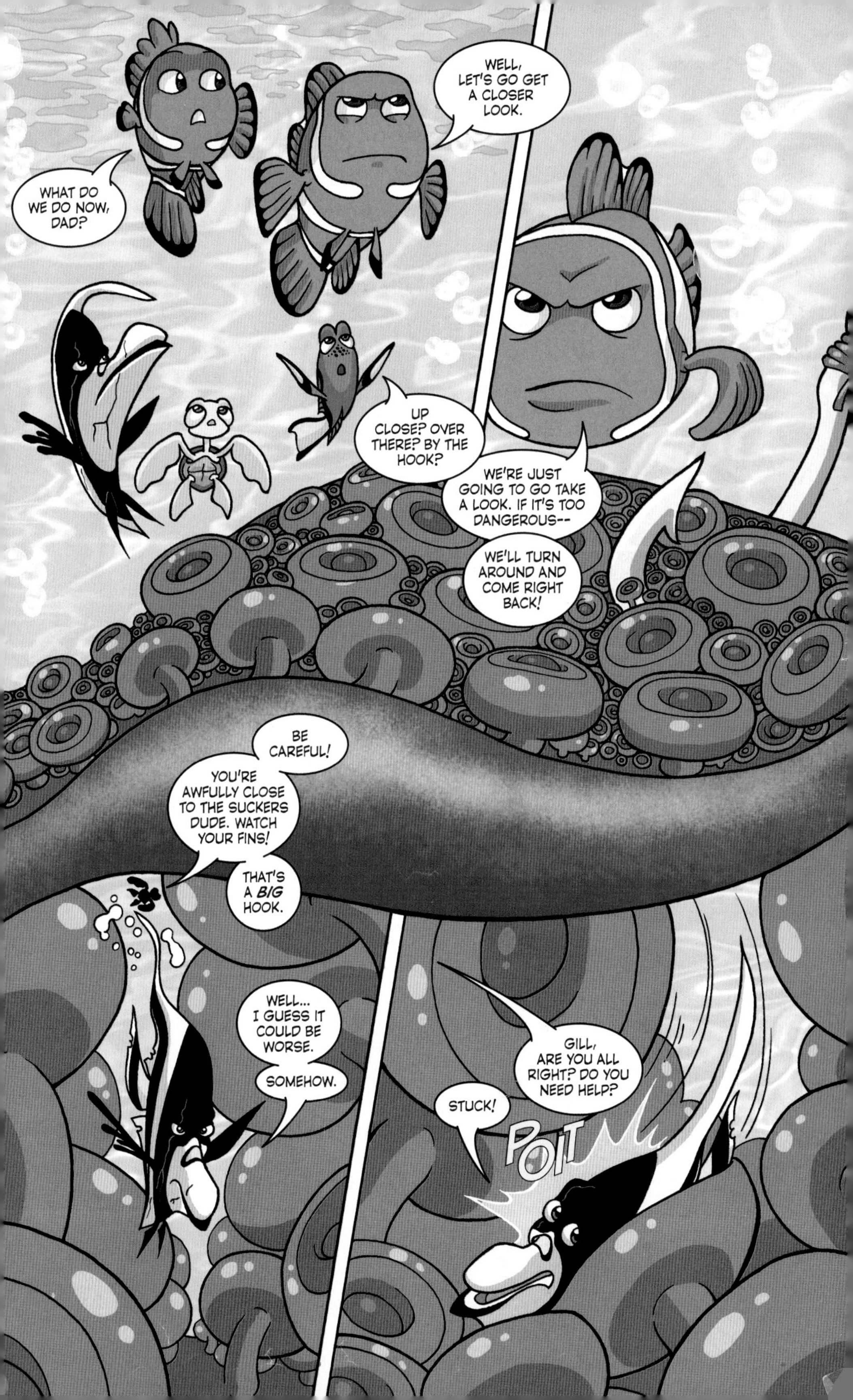
WHAT DO WE DO NOW, DAD?
WELL, LET'S GO GET A CLOSER LOOK.
UP CLOSE? OVER THERE? BY THE HOOK?
WE'RE JUST GOING TO GO TAKE A LOOK. IF IT'S TOO DANGEROUS--
WE'LL TURN AROUND AND COME RIGHT BACK!
BE CAREFUL!
YOU'RE AWFULLY CLOSE TO THE SUCKERS DUDE. WATCH YOUR FINS!
THAT'S A *BIG* HOOK.
WELL... I GUESS IT COULD BE WORSE.
SOMEHOW.
GILL, ARE YOU ALL RIGHT? DO YOU NEED HELP?
STUCK!
POIT

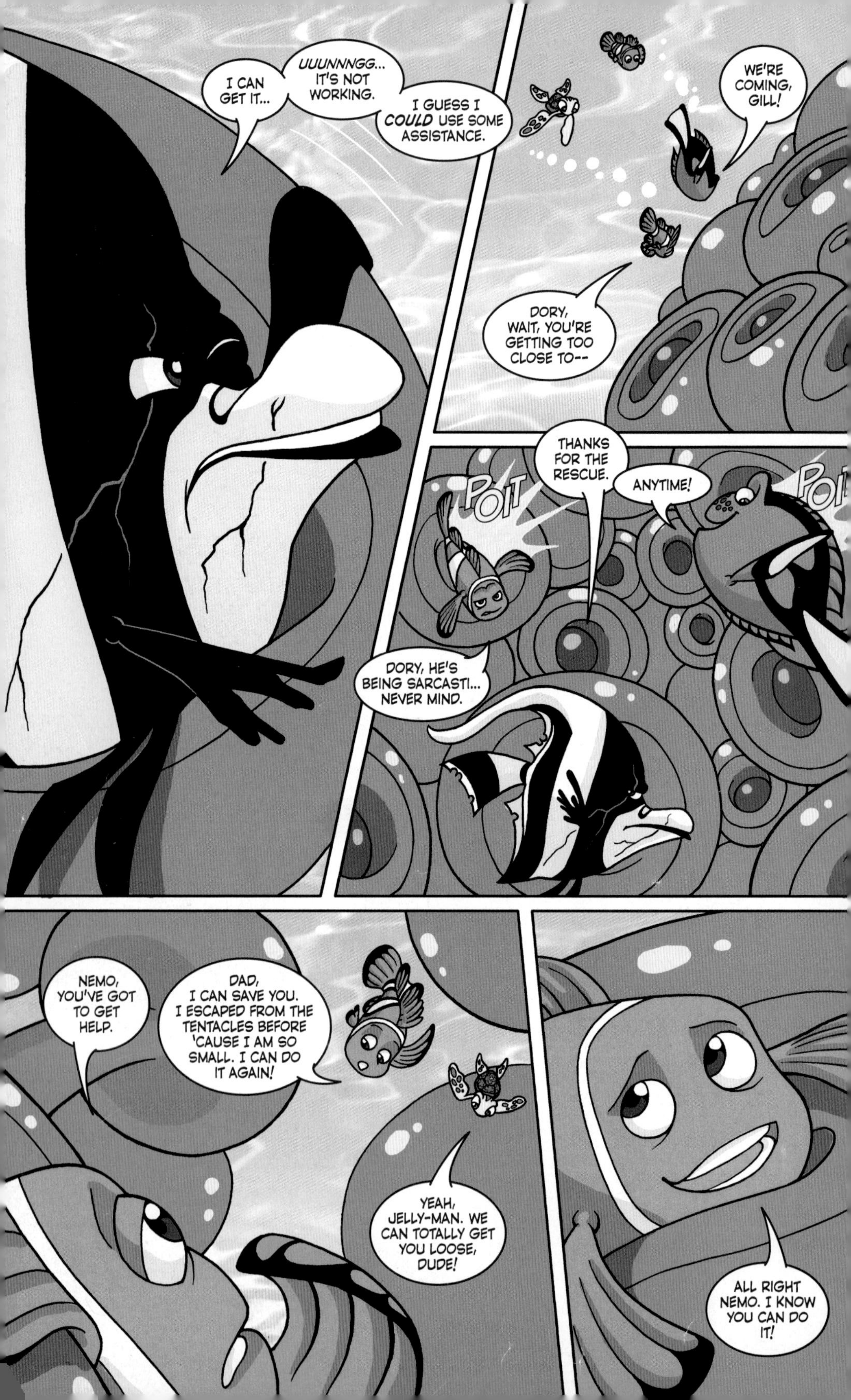
I CAN GET IT...
UUUNNNGG... IT'S NOT WORKING.
I GUESS I COULD USE SOME ASSISTANCE.
WE'RE COMING, GILL!
DORY, WAIT, YOU'RE GETTING TOO CLOSE TO--
POIT
THANKS FOR THE RESCUE.
ANYTIME!
POIT
DORY, HE'S BEING SARCASTI... NEVER MIND.
NEMO, YOU'VE GOT TO GET HELP.
DAD, I CAN SAVE YOU. I ESCAPED FROM THE TENTACLES BEFORE 'CAUSE I AM SO SMALL. I CAN DO IT AGAIN!
YEAH, JELLY-MAN. WE CAN TOTALLY GET YOU LOOSE, DUDE!
ALL RIGHT NEMO. I KNOW YOU CAN DO IT!

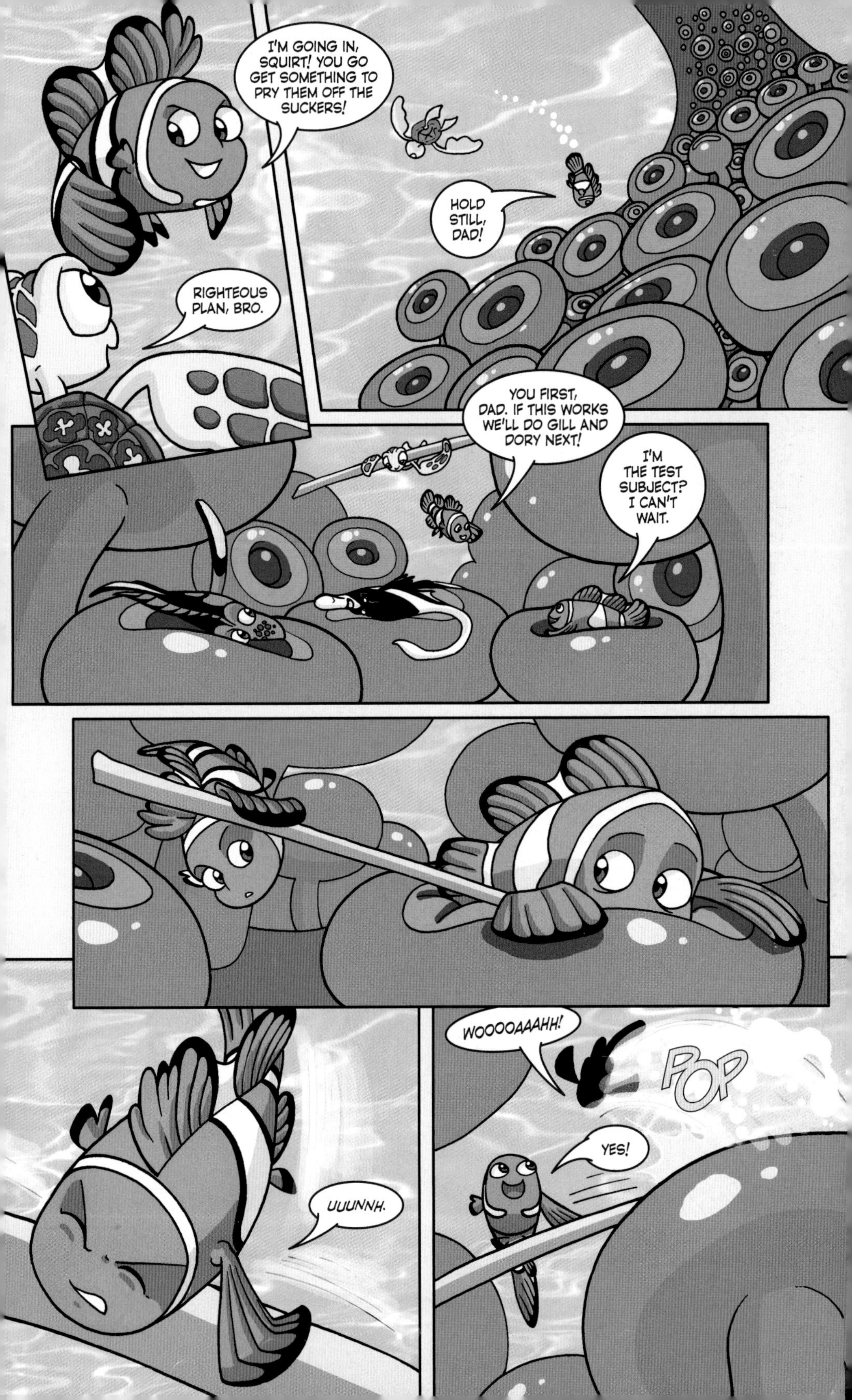
I'M GOING IN, SQUIRT! YOU GO GET SOMETHING TO PRY THEM OFF THE SUCKERS!
RIGHTEOUS PLAN, BRO.
HOLD STILL, DAD!
YOU FIRST, DAD. IF THIS WORKS WE'LL DO GILL AND DORY NEXT!
I'M THE TEST SUBJECT? I CAN'T WAIT.
UUUNNH.
WOOOOAAAHH!
POP
YES!

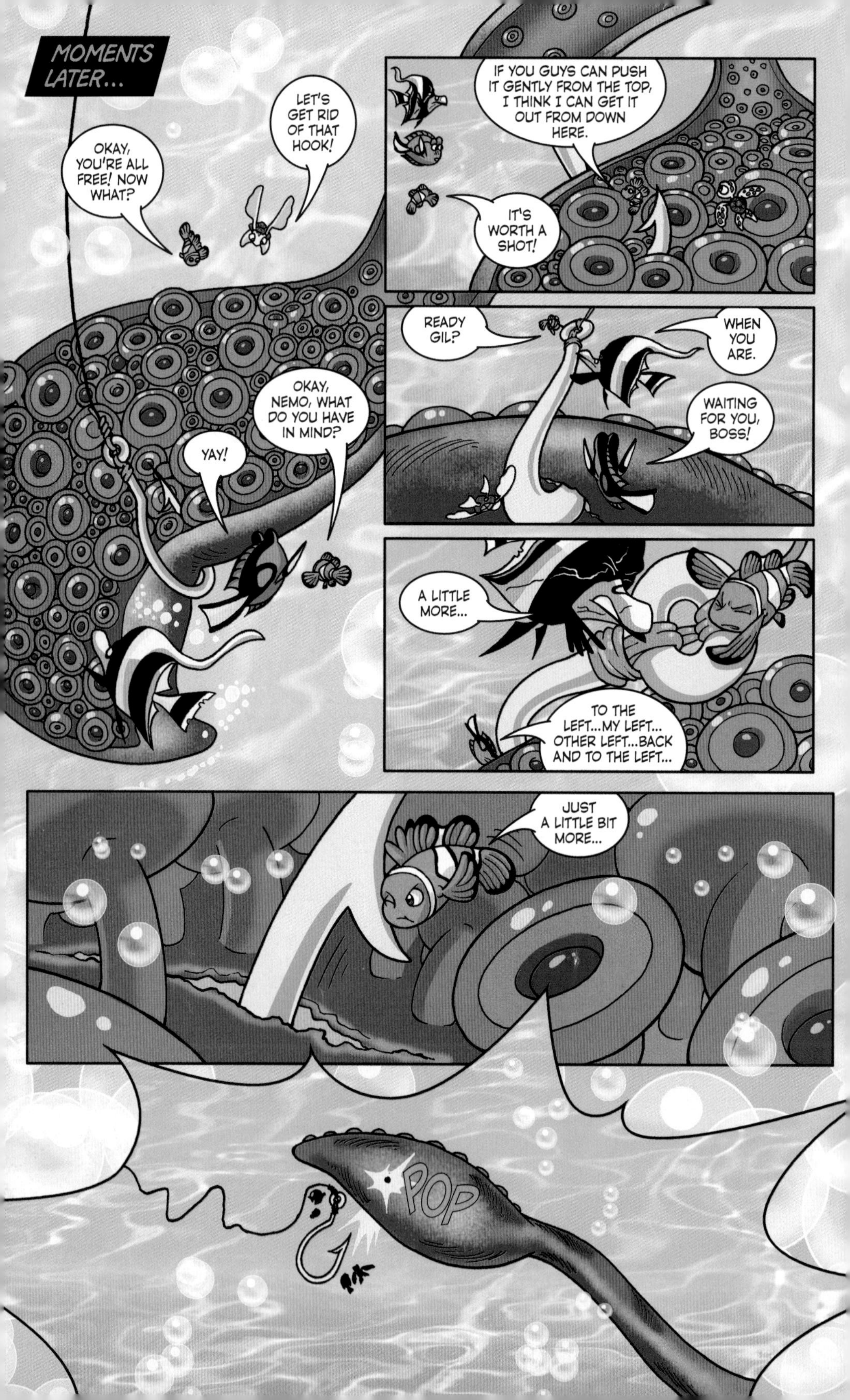
MOMENTS LATER...
OKAY, YOU'RE ALL FREE! NOW WHAT?
LET'S GET RID OF THAT HOOK!
IF YOU GUYS CAN PUSH IT GENTLY FROM THE TOP, I THINK I CAN GET IT OUT FROM DOWN HERE.
IT'S WORTH A SHOT!
YAY!
OKAY, NEMO, WHAT DO YOU HAVE IN MIND?
READY GIL?
WHEN YOU ARE.
WAITING FOR YOU, BOSS!
A LITTLE MORE...
TO THE LEFT...MY LEFT... OTHER LEFT...BACK AND TO THE LEFT...
JUST A LITTLE BIT MORE...
POP

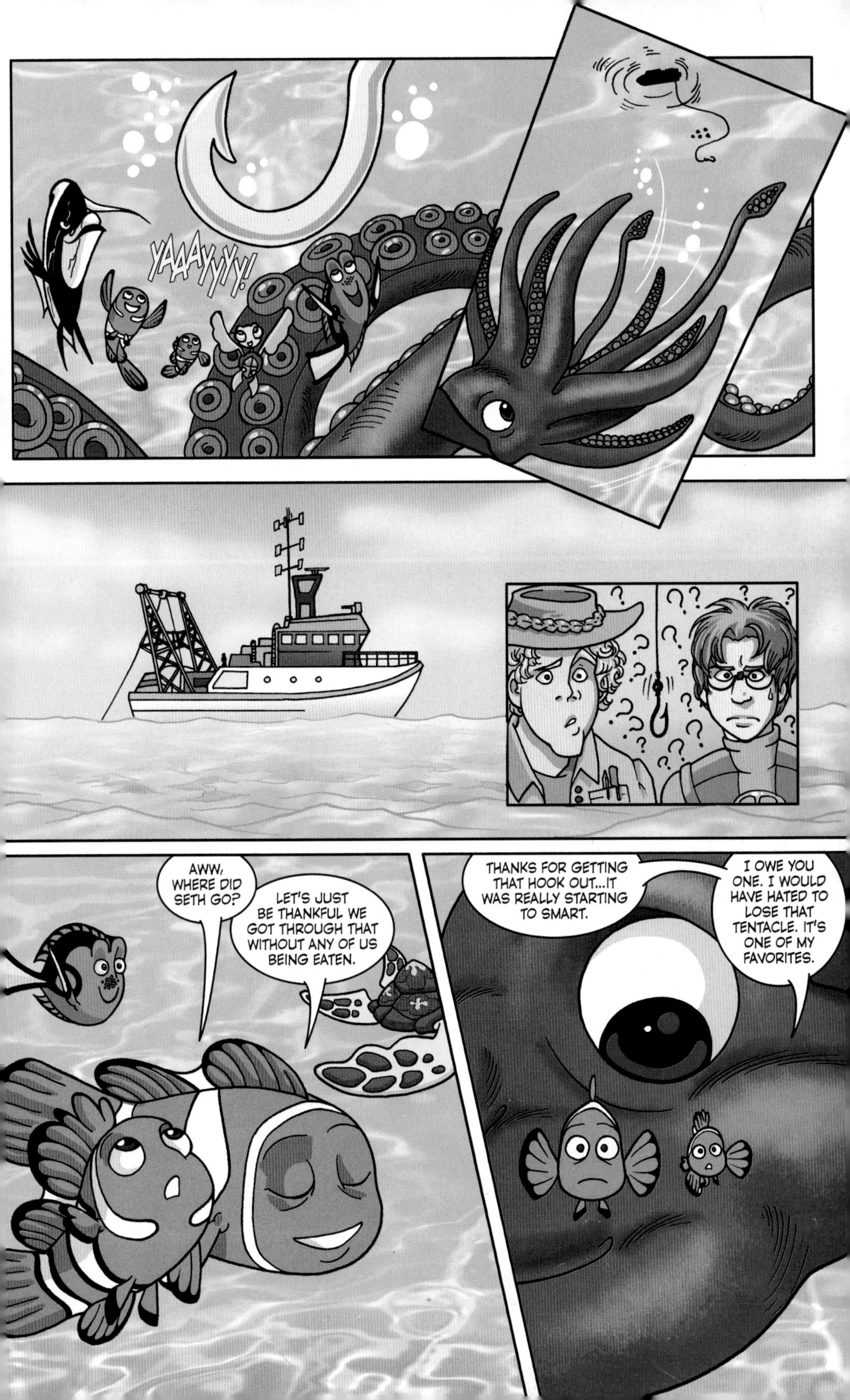
YAAAYYYY!
AWW, WHERE DID SETH GO?
LET'S JUST BE THANKFUL WE GOT THROUGH THAT WITHOUT ANY OF US BEING EATEN.
THANKS FOR GETTING THAT HOOK OUT...IT WAS REALLY STARTING TO SMART.
I OWE YOU ONE. I WOULD HAVE HATED TO LOSE THAT TENTACLE. IT'S ONE OF MY FAVORITES.

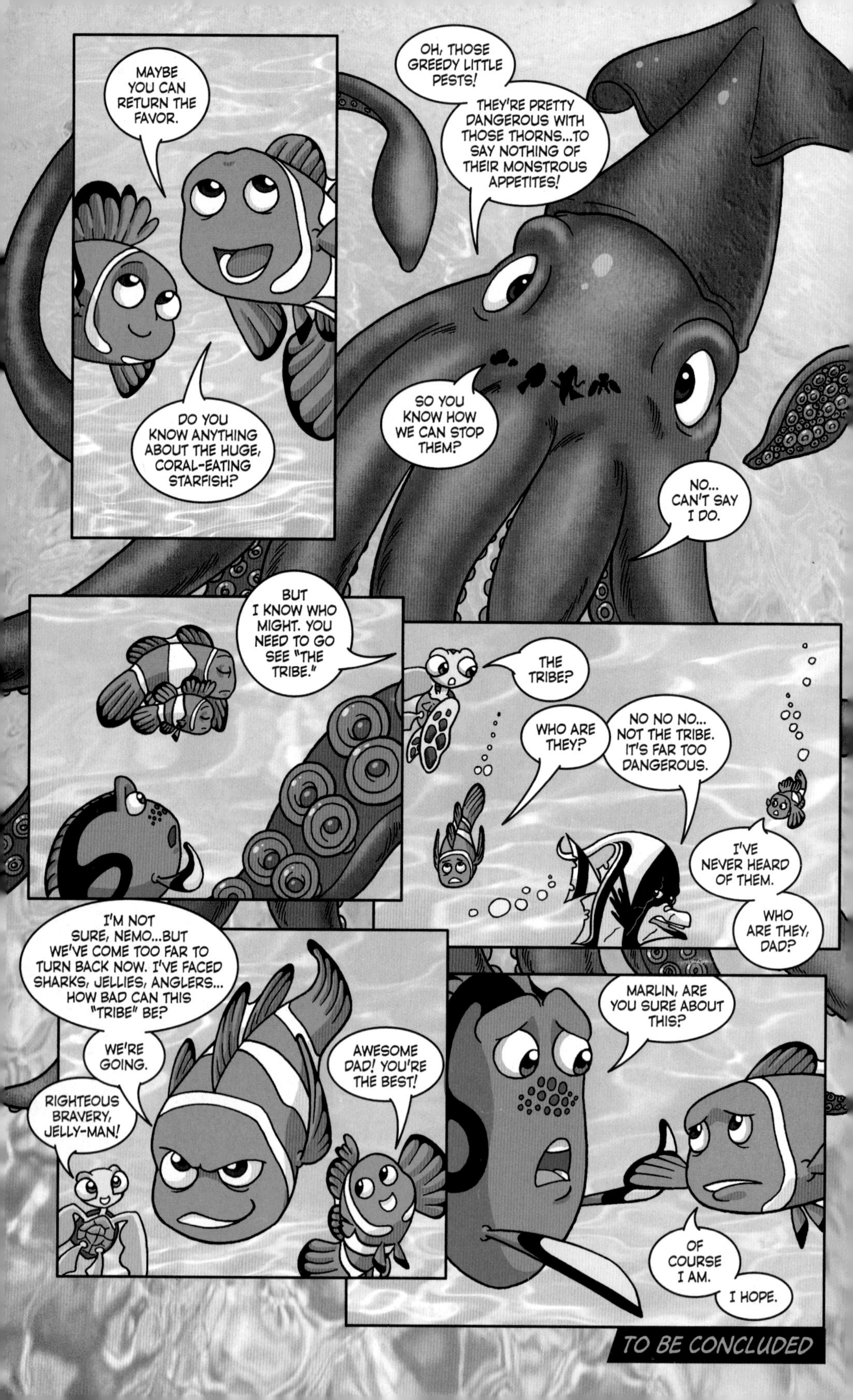
MAYBE YOU CAN RETURN THE FAVOR.
DO YOU KNOW ANYTHING ABOUT THE HUGE, CORAL-EATING STARFISH?
OH, THOSE GREEDY LITTLE PESTS!
THEY'RE PRETTY DANGEROUS WITH THOSE THORNS...TO SAY NOTHING OF THEIR MONSTROUS APPETITES!
SO YOU KNOW HOW WE CAN STOP THEM?
NO... CAN'T SAY I DO.
BUT I KNOW WHO MIGHT. YOU NEED TO GO SEE "THE TRIBE."
THE TRIBE?
WHO ARE THEY?
NO NO NO... NOT THE TRIBE. IT'S FAR TOO DANGEROUS.
I'VE NEVER HEARD OF THEM.
WHO ARE THEY, DAD?
I'M NOT SURE, NEMO...BUT WE'VE COME TOO FAR TO TURN BACK NOW. I'VE FACED SHARKS, JELLIES, ANGLERS... HOW BAD CAN THIS "TRIBE" BE?
WE'RE GOING.
RIGHTEOUS BRAVERY, JELLY-MAN!
AWESOME DAD! YOU'RE THE BEST!
MARLIN, ARE YOU SURE ABOUT THIS?
OF COURSE I AM.
I HOPE.
TO BE CONCLUDED

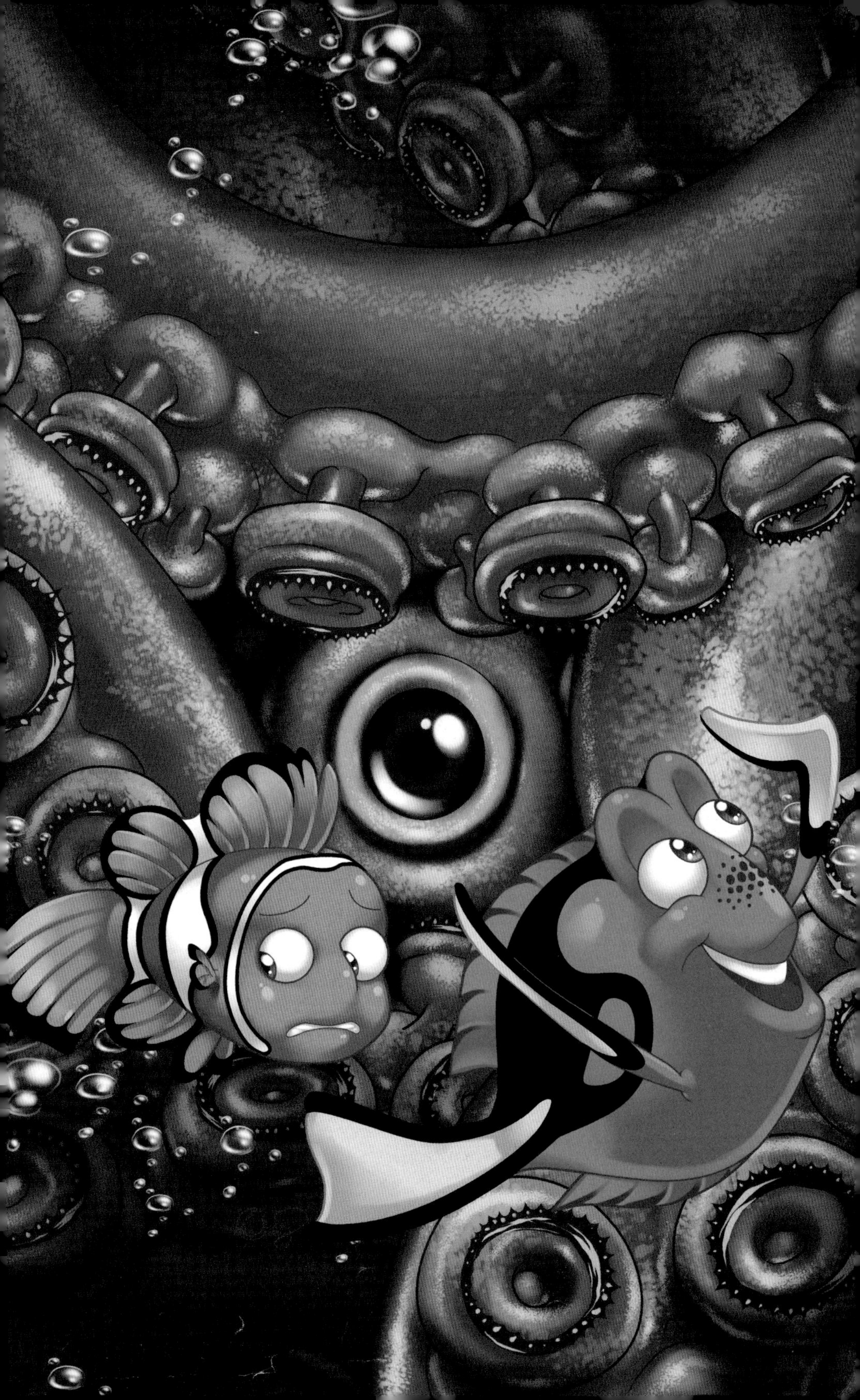

# CHAPTER FOUR

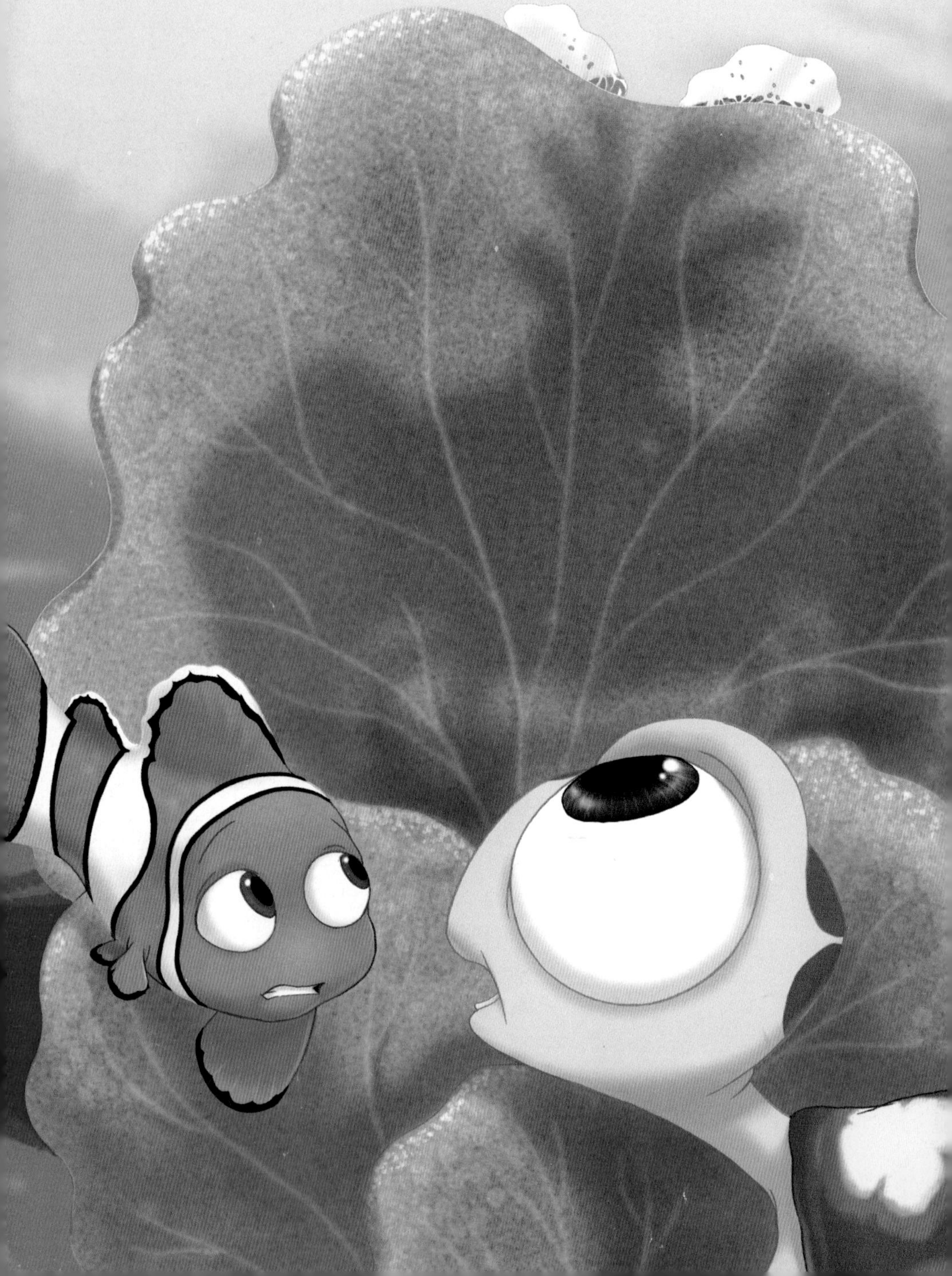

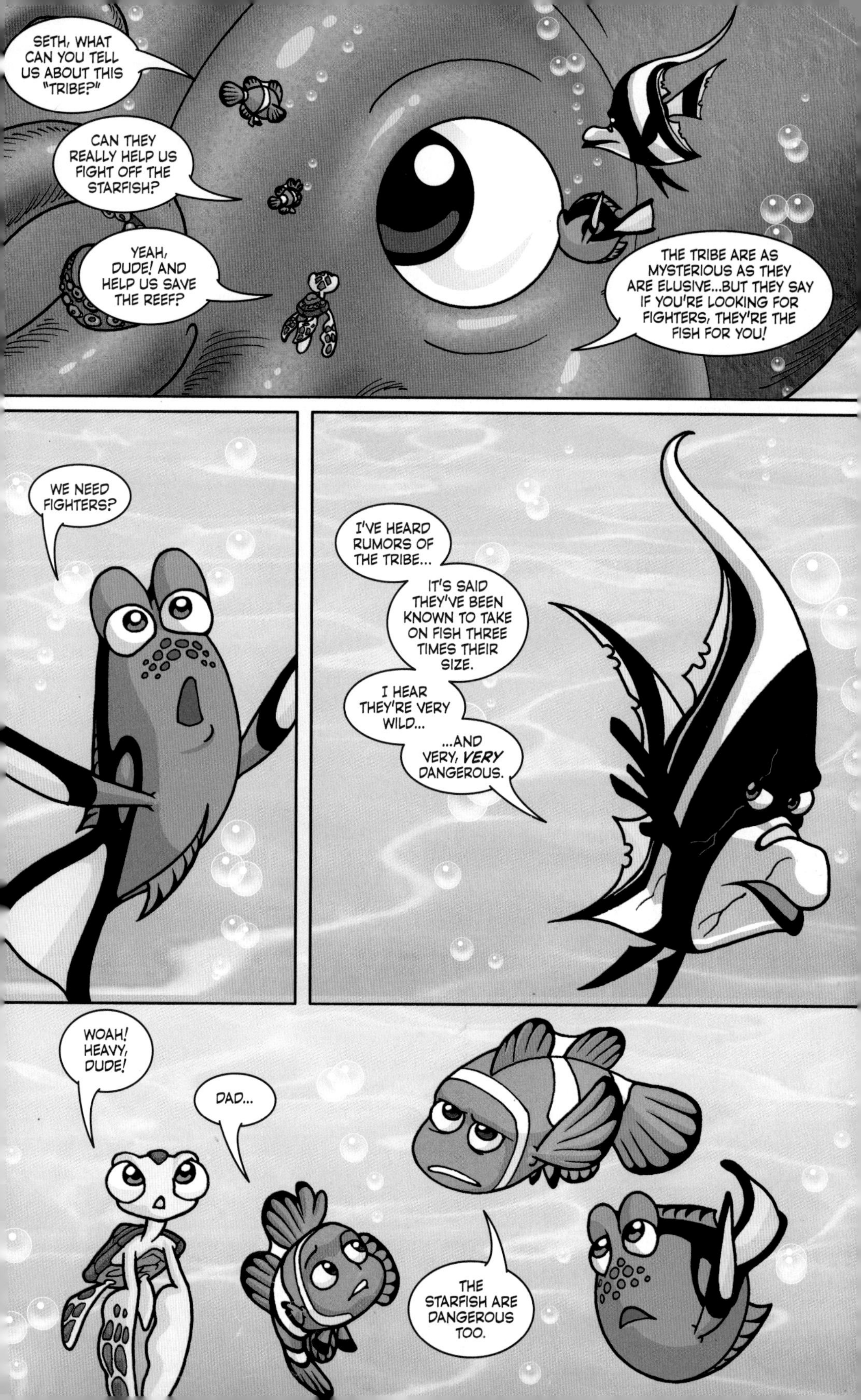
SETH, WHAT CAN YOU TELL US ABOUT THIS "TRIBE?"
CAN THEY REALLY HELP US FIGHT OFF THE STARFISH?
YEAH, DUDE! AND HELP US SAVE THE REEF?
THE TRIBE ARE AS MYSTERIOUS AS THEY ARE ELUSIVE...BUT THEY SAY IF YOU'RE LOOKING FOR FIGHTERS, THEY'RE THE FISH FOR YOU!
WE NEED FIGHTERS?
I'VE HEARD RUMORS OF THE TRIBE...
IT'S SAID THEY'VE BEEN KNOWN TO TAKE ON FISH THREE TIMES THEIR SIZE.
I HEAR THEY'RE VERY WILD...
...AND VERY, *VERY* DANGEROUS.
WOAH! HEAVY, DUDE!
DAD...
THE STARFISH ARE DANGEROUS TOO.

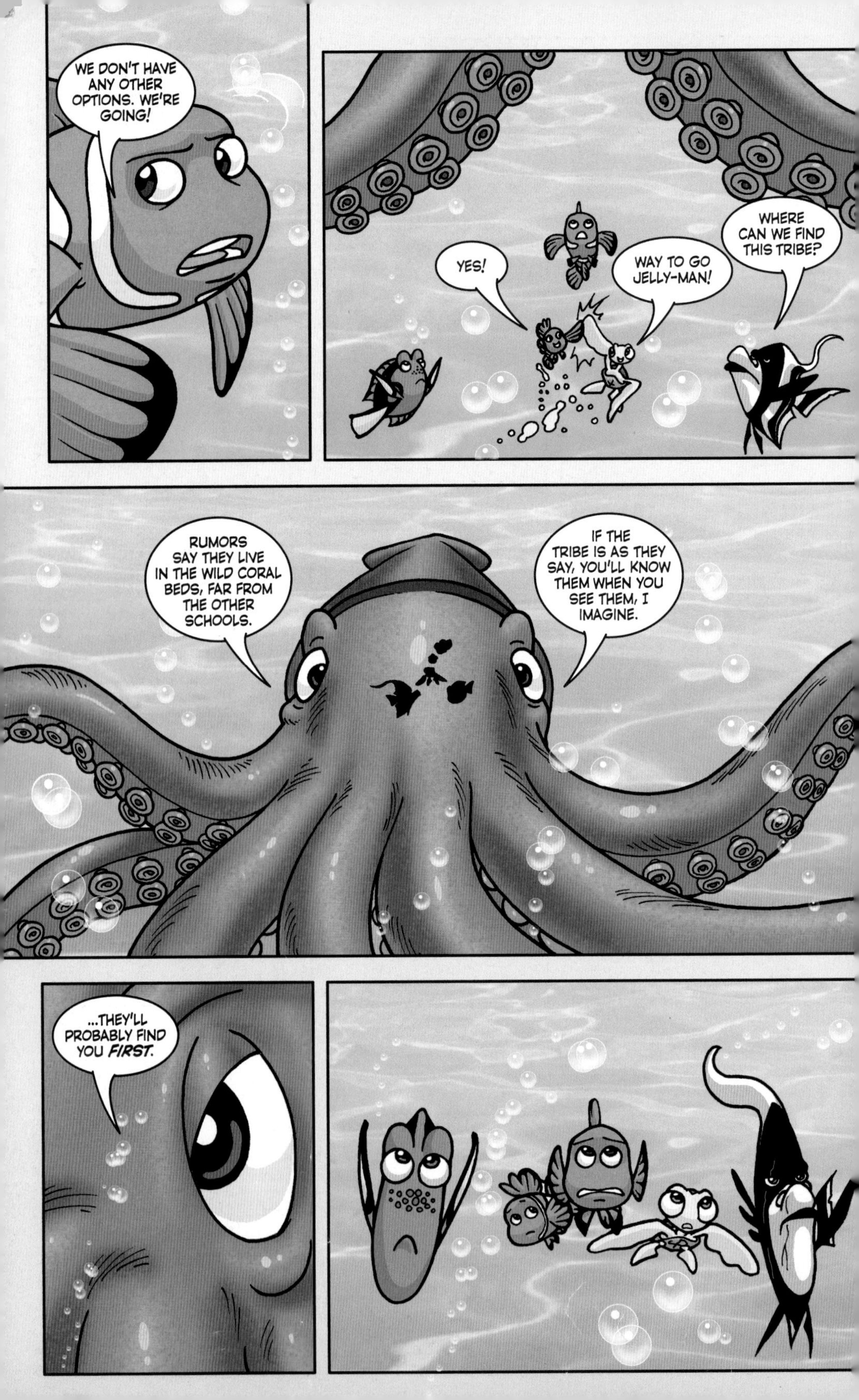
WE DON'T HAVE ANY OTHER OPTIONS. WE'RE GOING!
YES!
WAY TO GO JELLY-MAN!
WHERE CAN WE FIND THIS TRIBE?
RUMORS SAY THEY LIVE IN THE WILD CORAL BEDS, FAR FROM THE OTHER SCHOOLS.
IF THE TRIBE IS AS THEY SAY, YOU'LL KNOW THEM WHEN YOU SEE THEM, I IMAGINE.
...THEY'LL PROBABLY FIND YOU *FIRST*.

JUST REMEMBER, LITTLE FISH...
...IF YOU EVER NEED ME...
...I'LL BE HERE.
DEEP DOWN HERE...
BYE SETH!
DON'T FORGET TO WRITE!!
WHAT?!

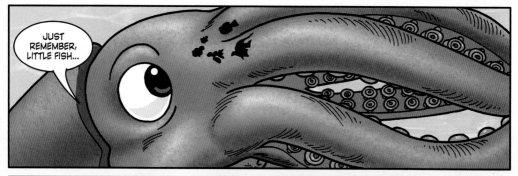

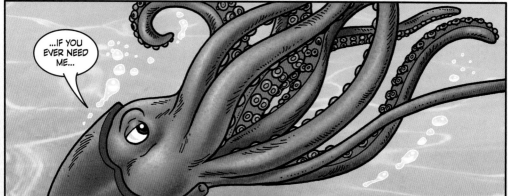

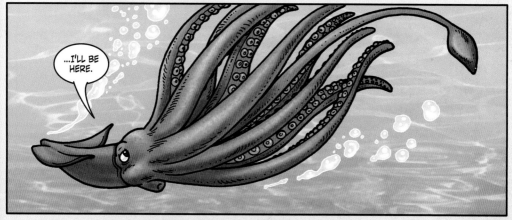

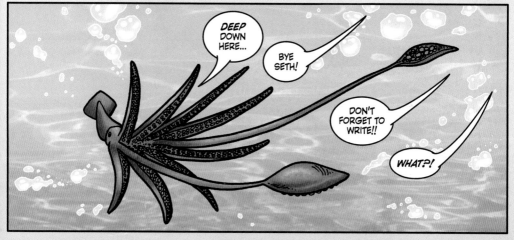

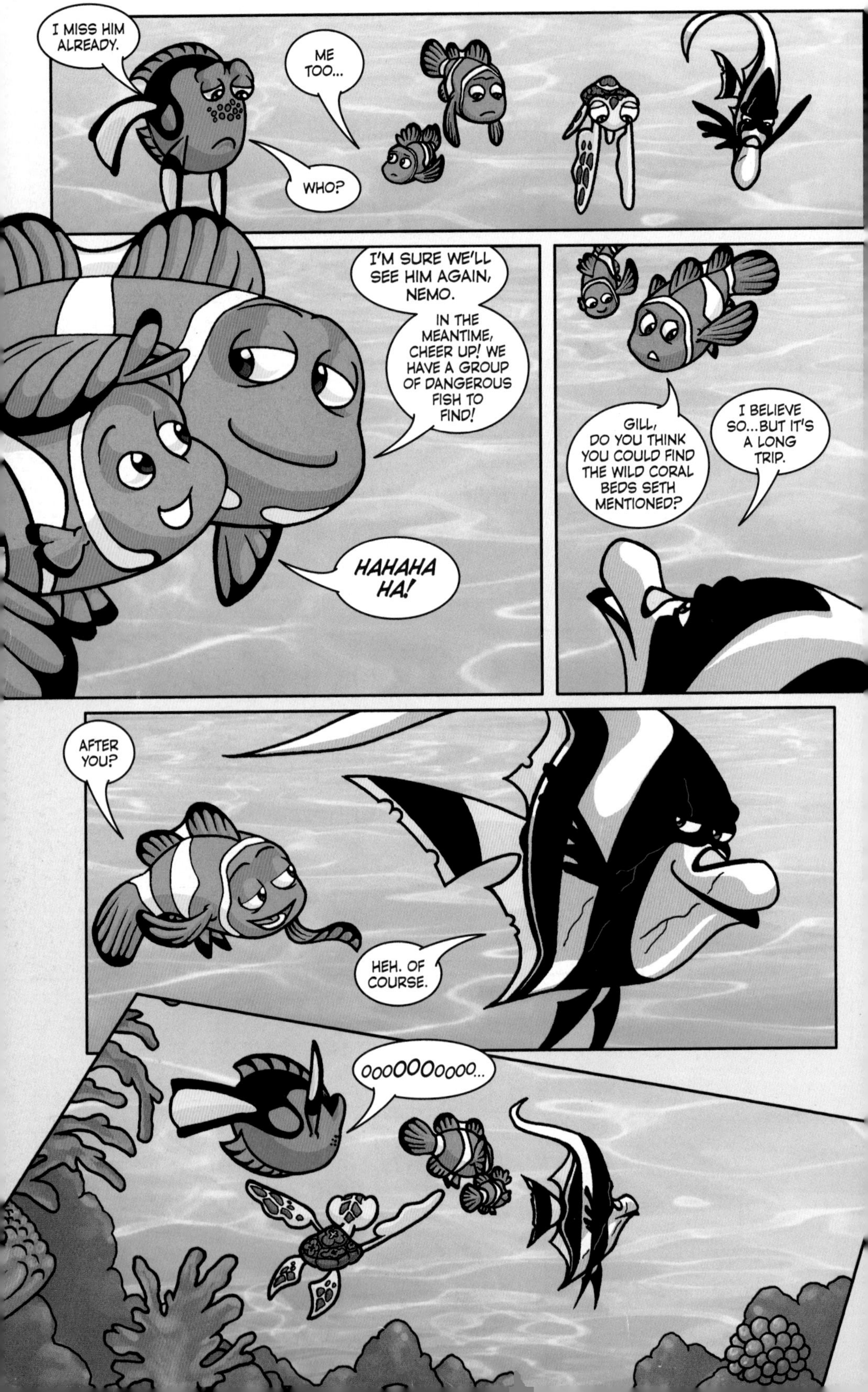
I MISS HIM ALREADY.
ME TOO...
WHO?
I'M SURE WE'LL SEE HIM AGAIN, NEMO.
IN THE MEANTIME, CHEER UP! WE HAVE A GROUP OF DANGEROUS FISH TO FIND!
HAHAHA HA!
GILL, DO YOU THINK YOU COULD FIND THE WILD CORAL BEDS SETH MENTIONED?
I BELIEVE SO...BUT IT'S A LONG TRIP.
AFTER YOU?
HEH. OF COURSE.
oooOOOoooo...

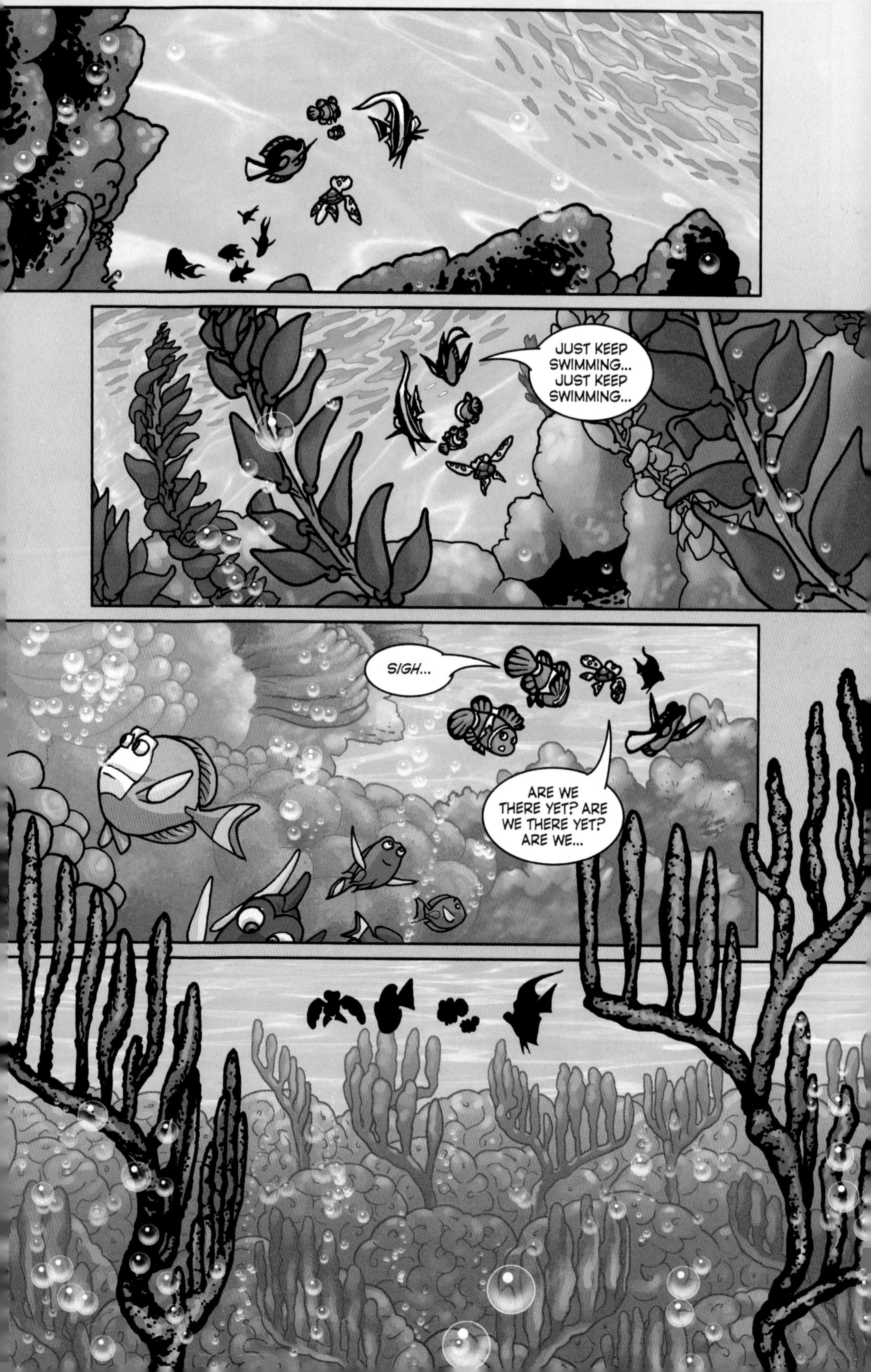
JUST KEEP SWIMMING... JUST KEEP SWIMMING...
SIGH...
ARE WE THERE YET? ARE WE THERE YET? ARE WE...

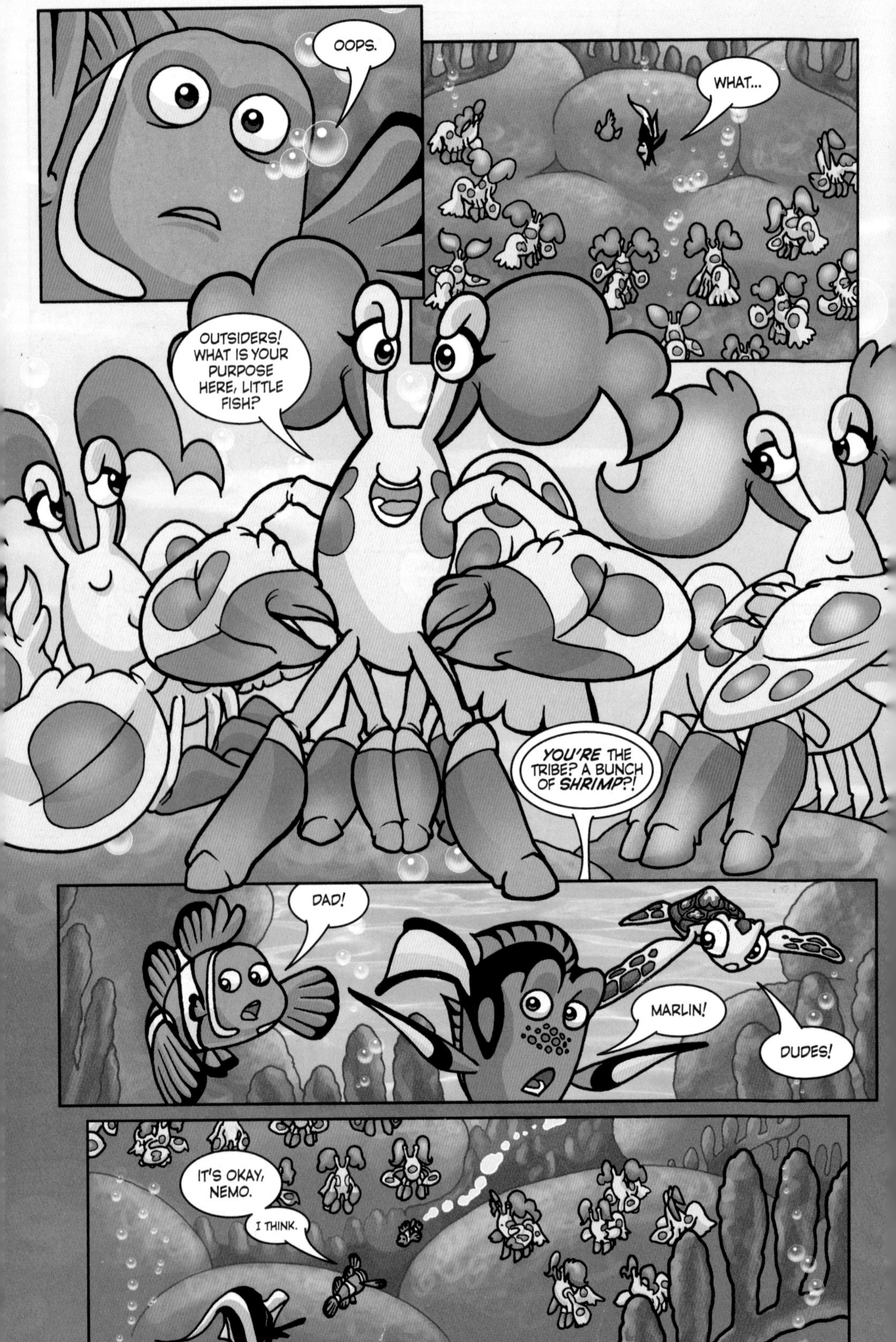
OOPS.
WHAT...
OUTSIDERS! WHAT IS YOUR PURPOSE HERE, LITTLE FISH?
YOU'RE THE TRIBE? A BUNCH OF SHRIMP?!
DAD!
MARLIN!
DUDES!
IT'S OKAY, NEMO.
I THINK.

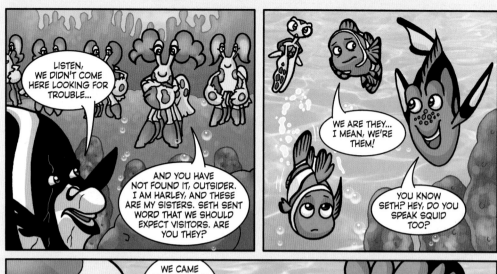

LISTEN, WE DIDN'T COME HERE LOOKING FOR TROUBLE...

AND YOU HAVE NOT FOUND IT, OUTSIDER. I AM HARLEY, AND THESE ARE MY SISTERS. SETH SENT WORD THAT WE SHOULD EXPECT VISITORS. ARE YOU THEY?

WE ARE THEY... I MEAN, WE'RE THEM!

YOU KNOW SETH? HEY, DO YOU SPEAK SQUID TOO?

WE CAME BECAUSE THE STARFISH ARE GOING TO EAT OUR CORAL REEF! CAN YOU HELP US SAVE OUR HOME?

YOU ASK MUCH OF US, SMALL ONE. COME WITH US. WE WILL HEAR OF YOUR PLIGHT ON THE WAY.

ON THE WAY?

CAN WE, DAD?

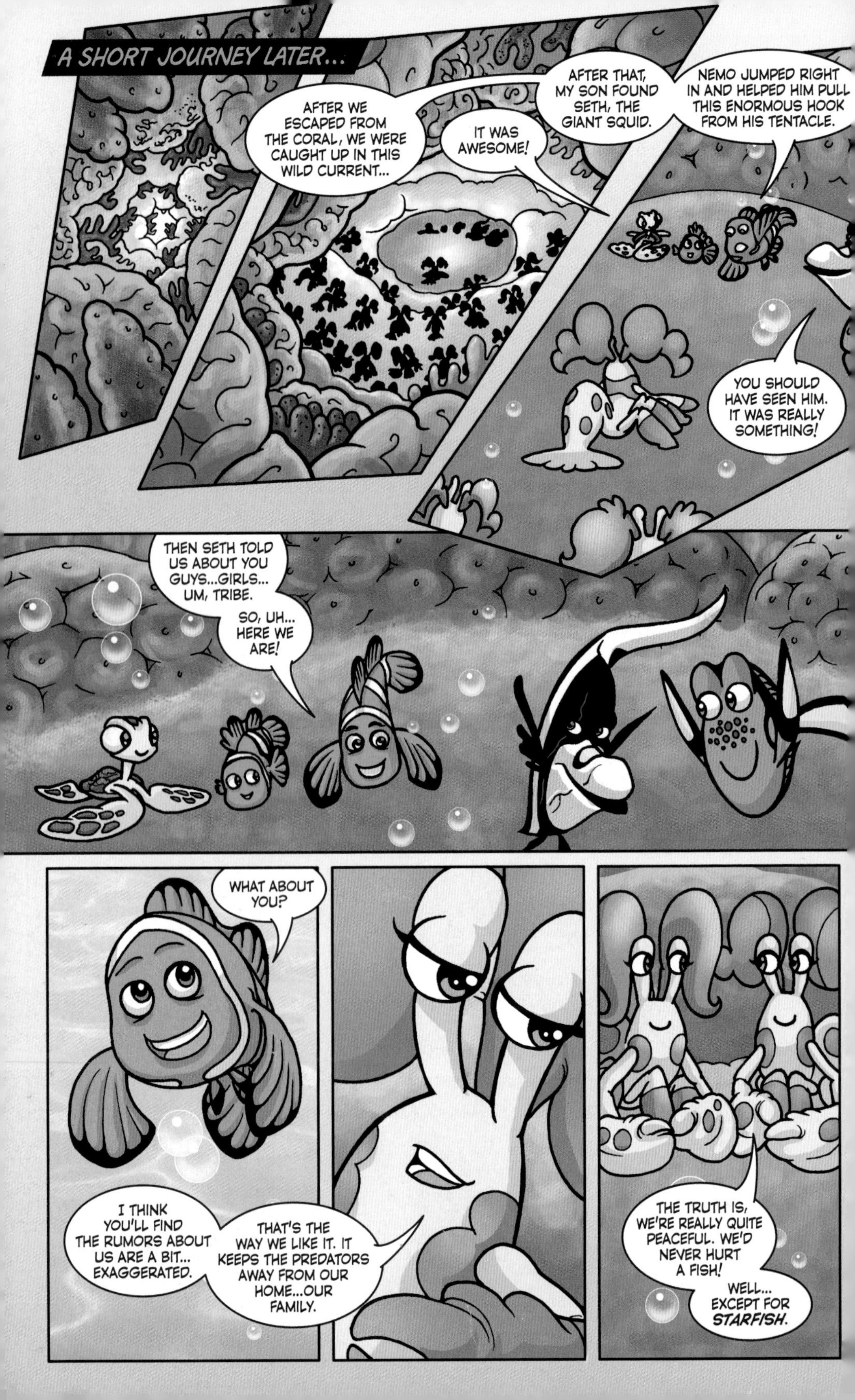
A SHORT JOURNEY LATER...
AFTER WE ESCAPED FROM THE CORAL, WE WERE CAUGHT UP IN THIS WILD CURRENT...
IT WAS AWESOME!
AFTER THAT, MY SON FOUND SETH, THE GIANT SQUID.
NEMO JUMPED RIGHT IN AND HELPED HIM PULL THIS ENORMOUS HOOK FROM HIS TENTACLE.
YOU SHOULD HAVE SEEN HIM. IT WAS REALLY SOMETHING!
THEN SETH TOLD US ABOUT YOU GUYS...GIRLS... UM, TRIBE.
SO, UH... HERE WE ARE!
WHAT ABOUT YOU?
I THINK YOU'LL FIND THE RUMORS ABOUT US ARE A BIT... EXAGGERATED.
THAT'S THE WAY WE LIKE IT. IT KEEPS THE PREDATORS AWAY FROM OUR HOME...OUR FAMILY.
THE TRUTH IS, WE'RE REALLY QUITE PEACEFUL. WE'D NEVER HURT A FISH!
WELL... EXCEPT FOR STARFISH.

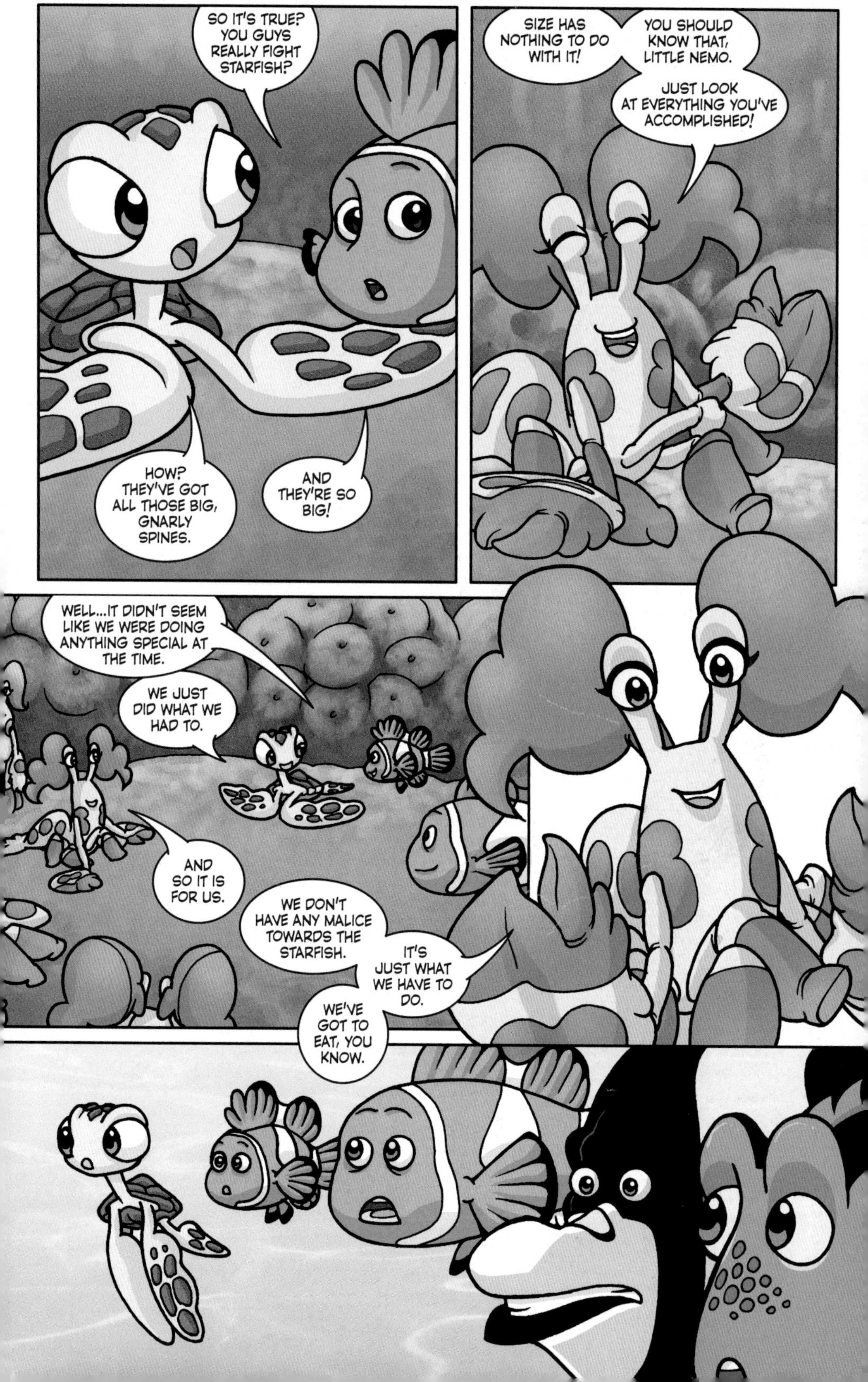

SO IT'S TRUE? YOU GUYS REALLY FIGHT STARFISH?
HOW? THEY'VE GOT ALL THOSE BIG, GNARLY SPINES.
AND THEY'RE SO BIG!
SIZE HAS NOTHING TO DO WITH IT!
YOU SHOULD KNOW THAT, LITTLE NEMO.
JUST LOOK AT EVERYTHING YOU'VE ACCOMPLISHED!
WELL...IT DIDN'T SEEM LIKE WE WERE DOING ANYTHING SPECIAL AT THE TIME.
WE JUST DID WHAT WE HAD TO.
AND SO IT IS FOR US.
WE DON'T HAVE ANY MALICE TOWARDS THE STARFISH.
IT'S JUST WHAT WE HAVE TO DO.
WE'VE GOT TO EAT, YOU KNOW.

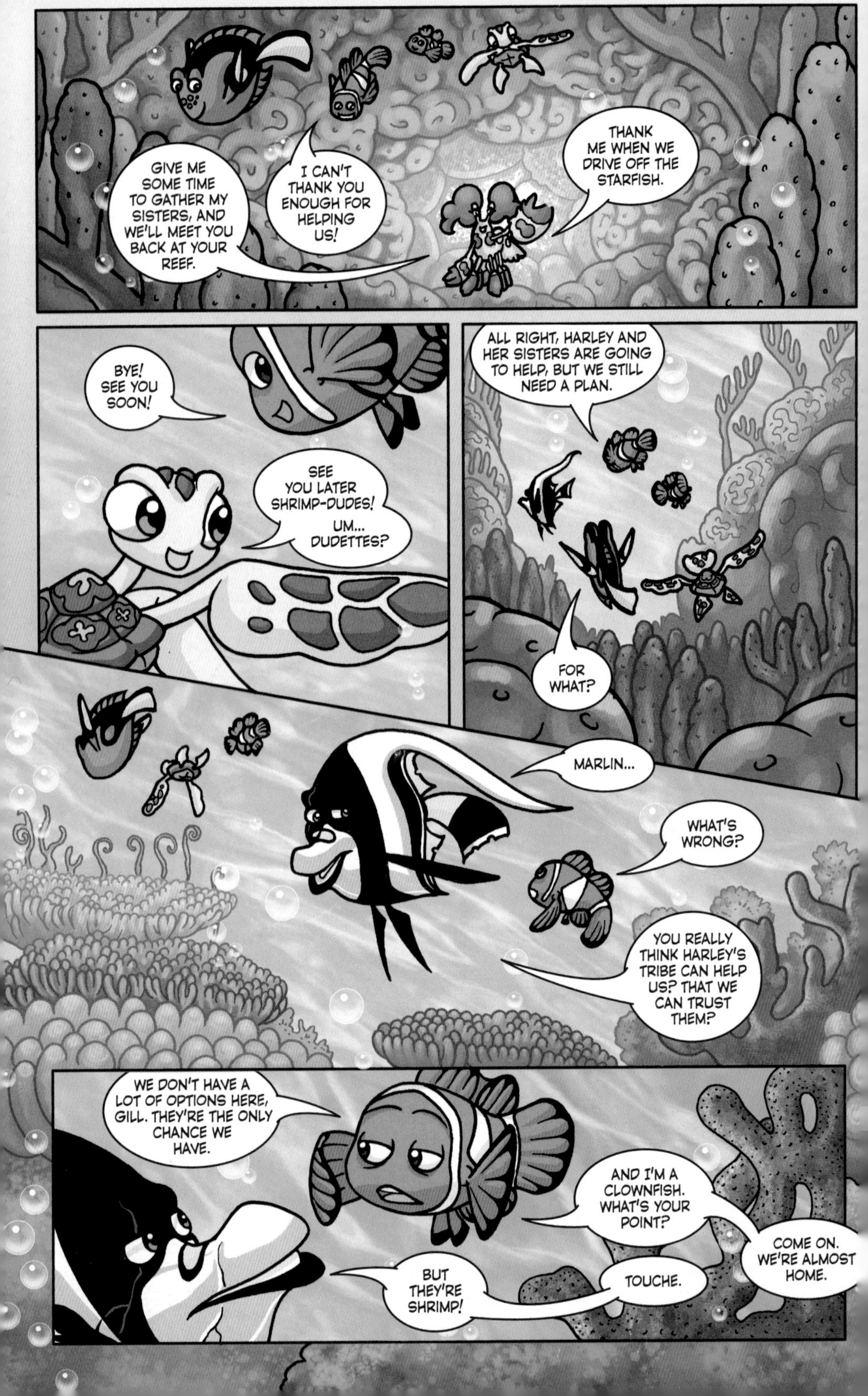
GIVE ME SOME TIME TO GATHER MY SISTERS, AND WE'LL MEET YOU BACK AT YOUR REEF.
I CAN'T THANK YOU ENOUGH FOR HELPING US!
THANK ME WHEN WE DRIVE OFF THE STARFISH.
BYE! SEE YOU SOON!
SEE YOU LATER SHRIMP-DUDES!
UM... DUDETTES?
ALL RIGHT, HARLEY AND HER SISTERS ARE GOING TO HELP, BUT WE STILL NEED A PLAN.
FOR WHAT?
MARLIN...
WHAT'S WRONG?
YOU REALLY THINK HARLEY'S TRIBE CAN HELP US? THAT WE CAN TRUST THEM?
WE DON'T HAVE A LOT OF OPTIONS HERE, GILL. THEY'RE THE ONLY CHANCE WE HAVE.
BUT THEY'RE SHRIMP!
AND I'M A CLOWNFISH. WHAT'S YOUR POINT?
TOUCHE.
COME ON. WE'RE ALMOST HOME.

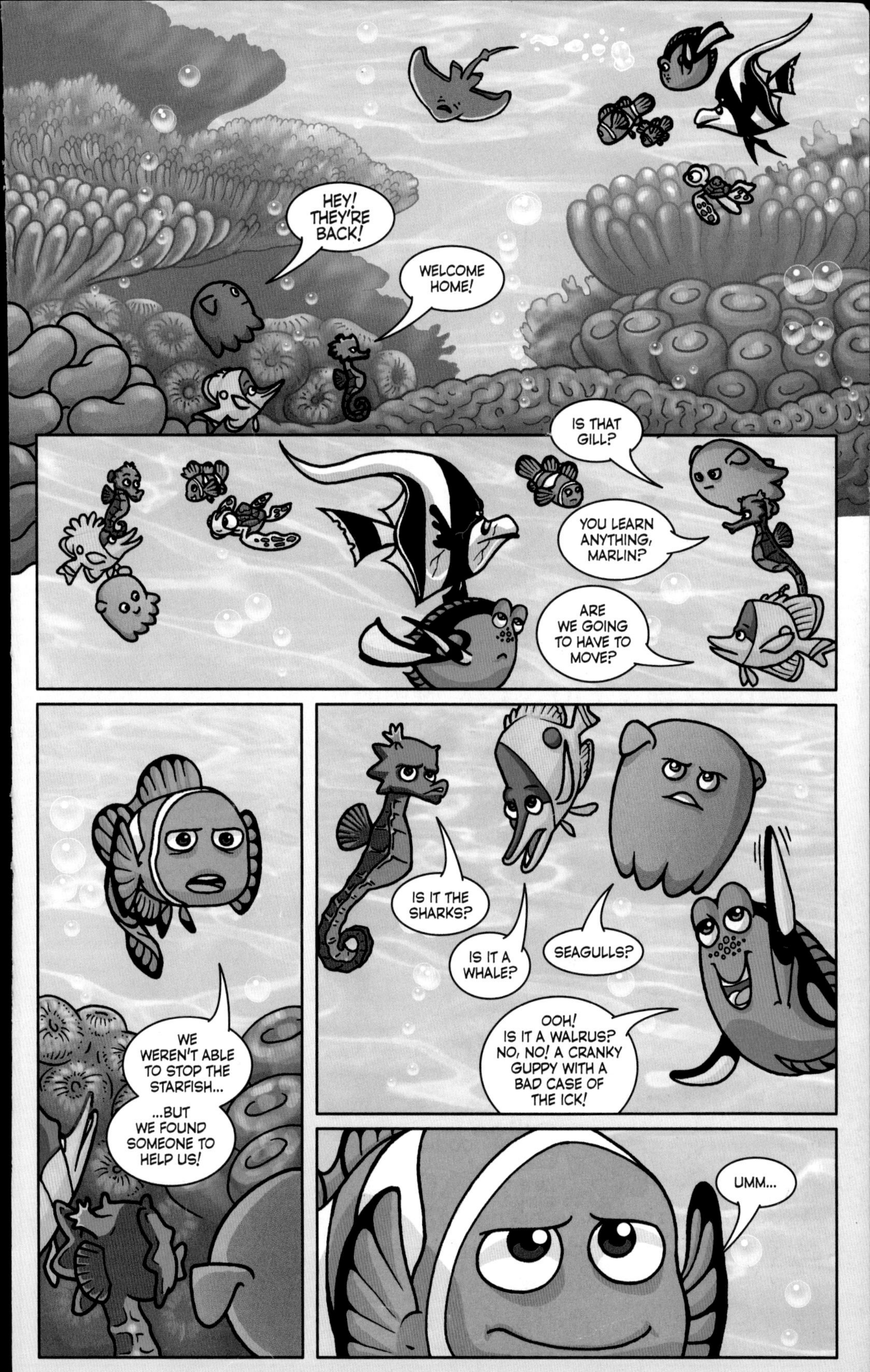
HEY! THEY'RE BACK!
WELCOME HOME!
IS THAT GILL?
YOU LEARN ANYTHING, MARLIN?
ARE WE GOING TO HAVE TO MOVE?
WE WEREN'T ABLE TO STOP THE STARFISH...
...BUT WE FOUND SOMEONE TO HELP US!
IS IT THE SHARKS?
IS IT A WHALE?
SEAGULLS?
OOH! IS IT A WALRUS? NO, NO! A CRANKY GUPPY WITH A BAD CASE OF THE ICK!
UMM...

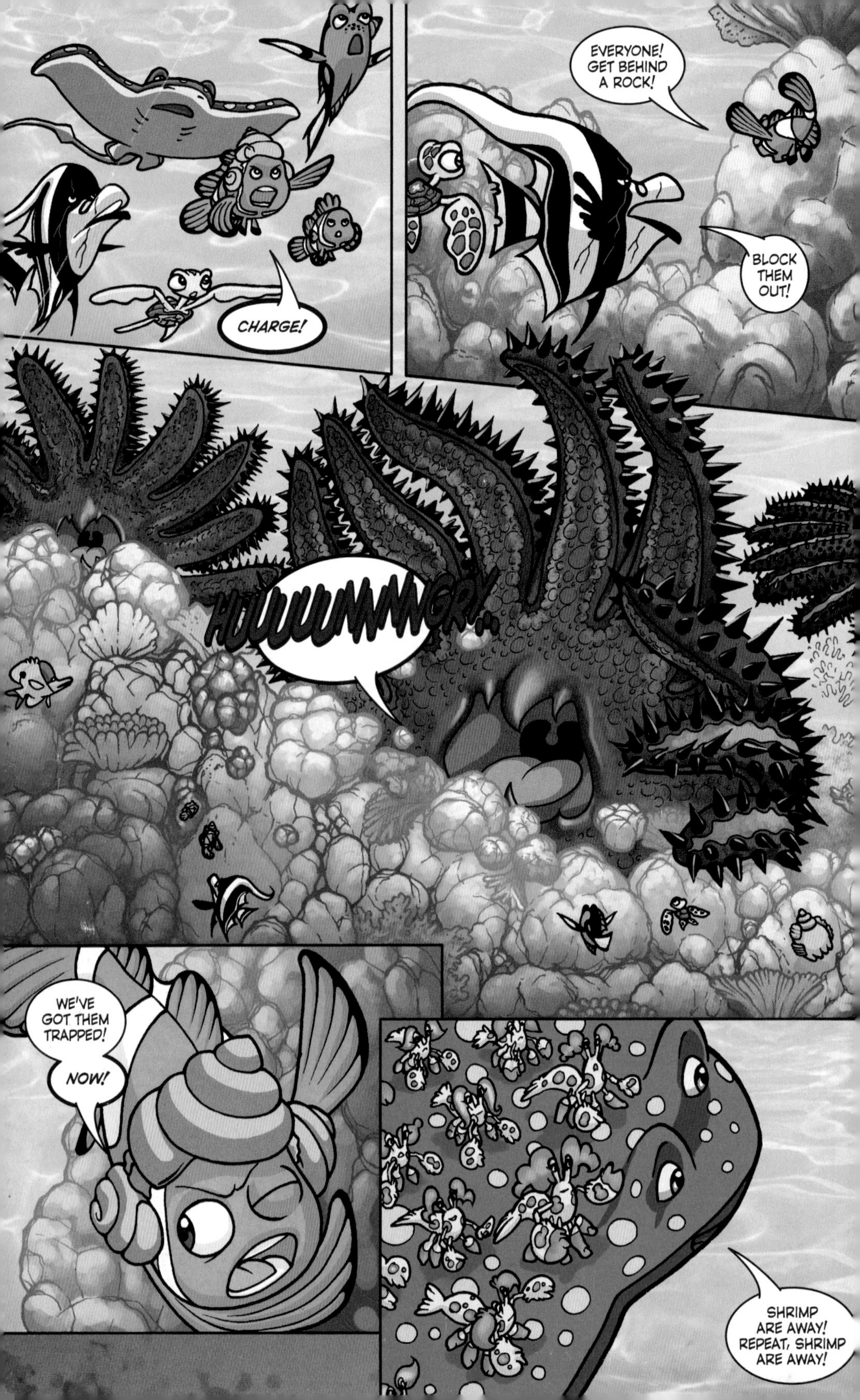
CHARGE!
EVERYONE! GET BEHIND A ROCK!
BLOCK THEM OUT!
HUUUUUNNNNGRY...
WE'VE GOT THEM TRAPPED!
NOW!
SHRIMP ARE AWAY! REPEAT, SHRIMP ARE AWAY!

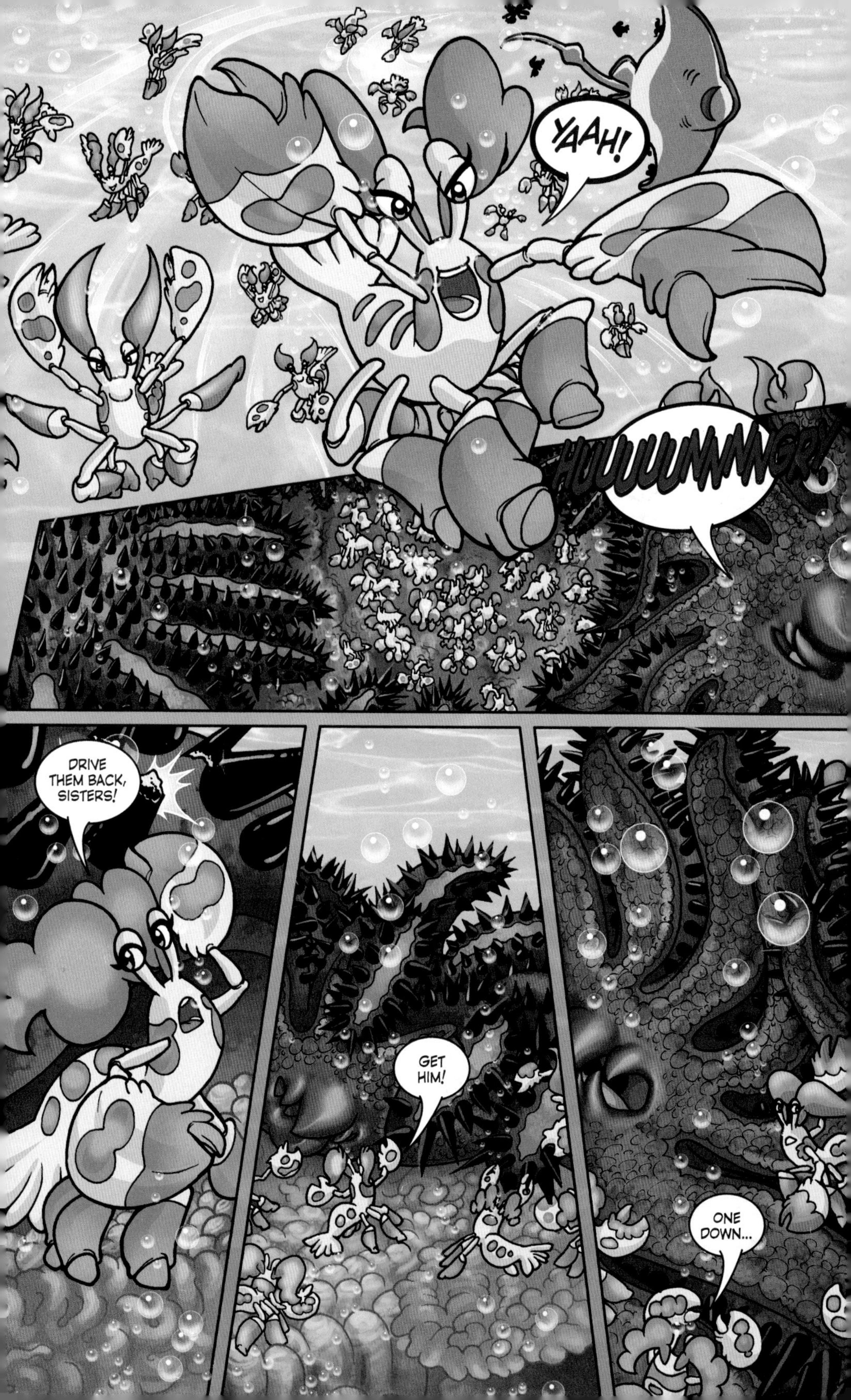
YAAH!
HUUUUUNNNNGR!
DRIVE THEM BACK, SISTERS!
GET HIM!
ONE DOWN...

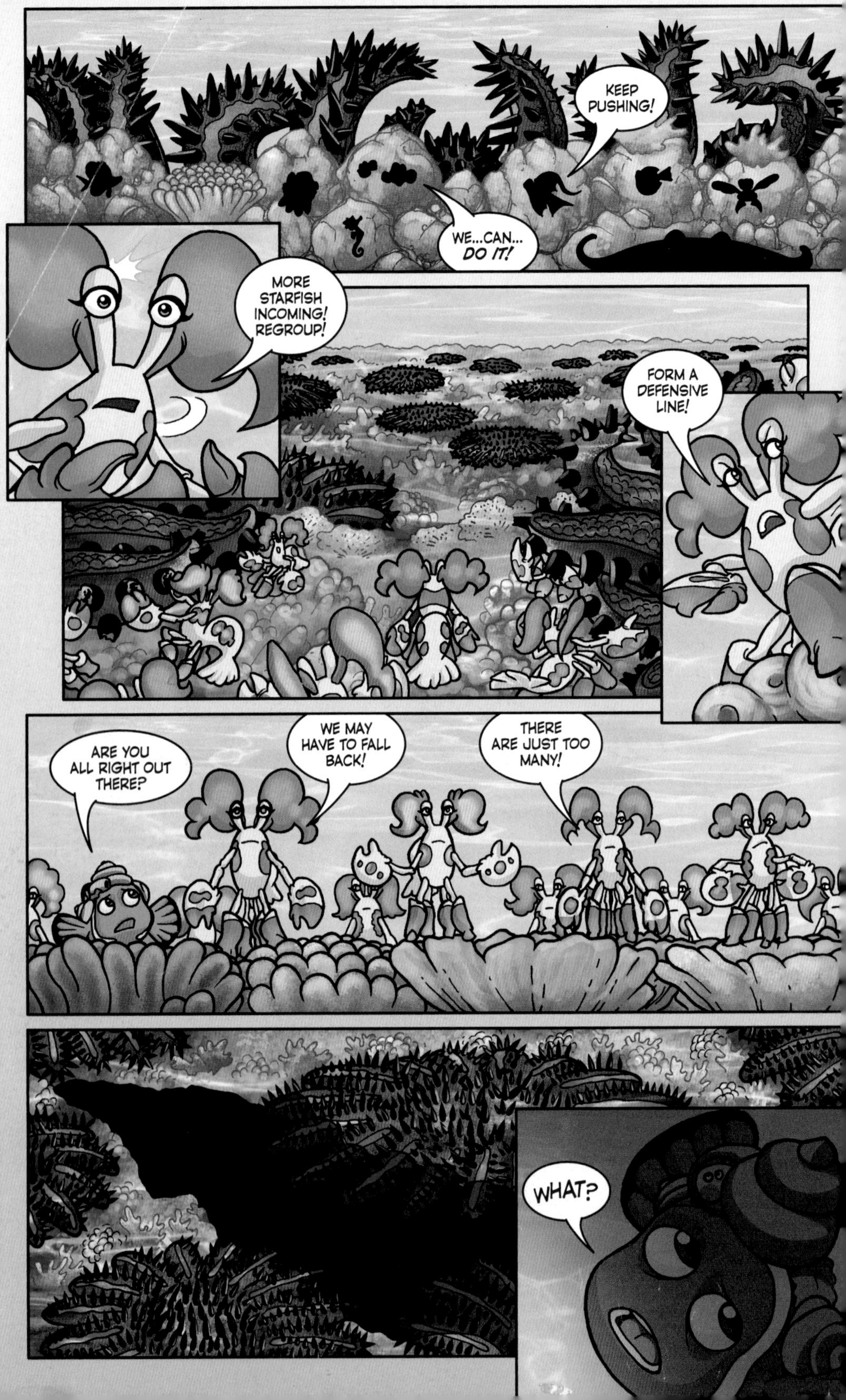
KEEP PUSHING!
WE...CAN... DO IT!
MORE STARFISH INCOMING! REGROUP!
FORM A DEFENSIVE LINE!
ARE YOU ALL RIGHT OUT THERE?
WE MAY HAVE TO FALL BACK!
THERE ARE JUST TOO MANY!
WHAT?

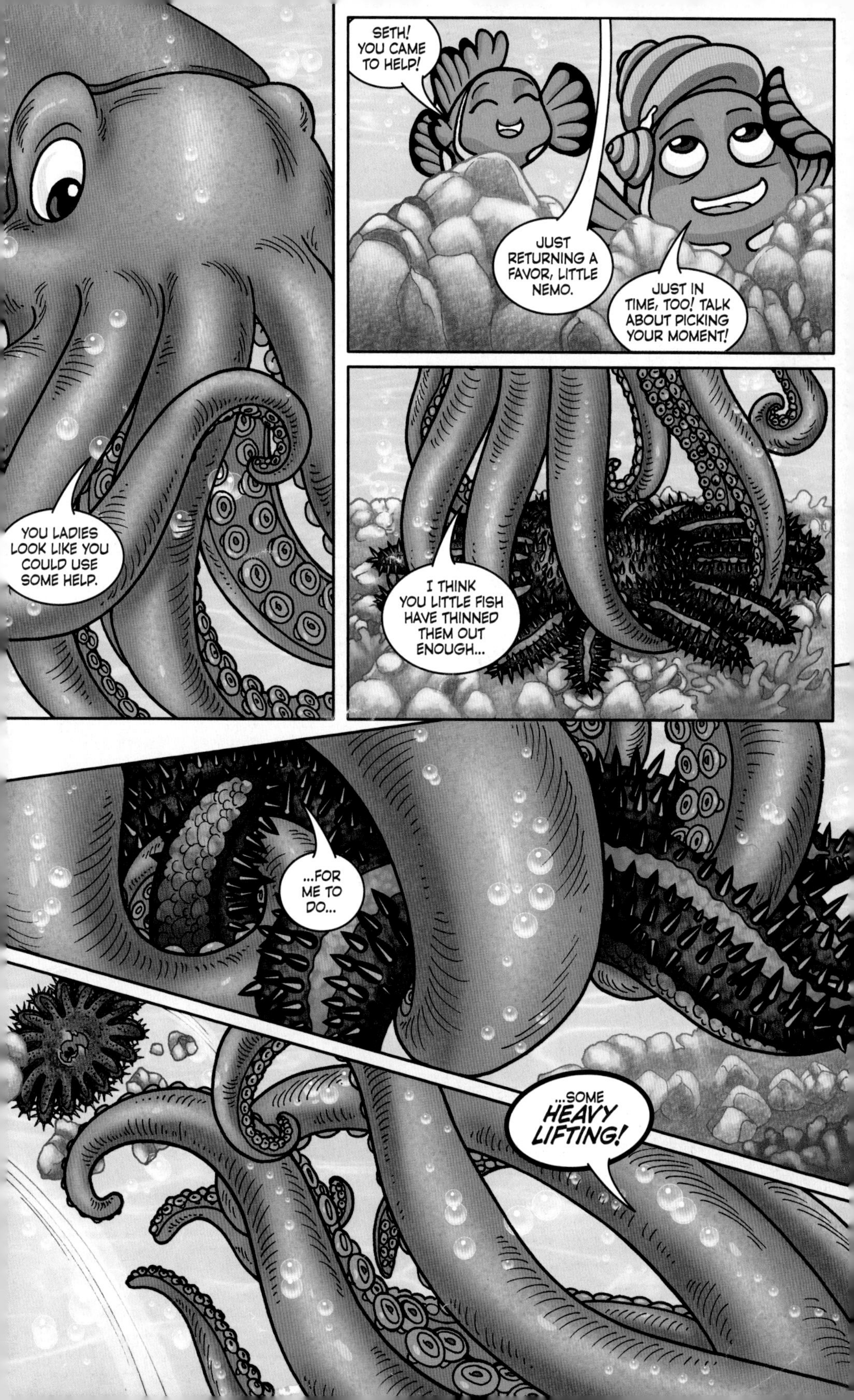
YOU LADIES LOOK LIKE YOU COULD USE SOME HELP.
SETH! YOU CAME TO HELP!
JUST RETURNING A FAVOR, LITTLE NEMO.
JUST IN TIME, TOO! TALK ABOUT PICKING YOUR MOMENT!
I THINK YOU LITTLE FISH HAVE THINNED THEM OUT ENOUGH...
...FOR ME TO DO...
...SOME HEAVY LIFTING!

YAAY!

GO SETH!!

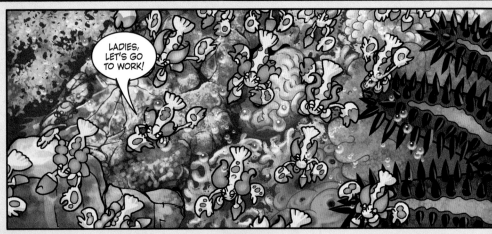

LADIES, LET'S GO TO WORK!

WOW.

AWESOME, DAD! WE DID IT!

LOOKS LIKE THE REEF IS SAFE.

WHAT'S LEFT OF IT, ANYWAY.

THAT WAS RADICAL! THE STARFISH WERE ALL "HUUUH" AND THE SHRIMP WERE ALL "YAAH"!

TOTALLY RADICAL!

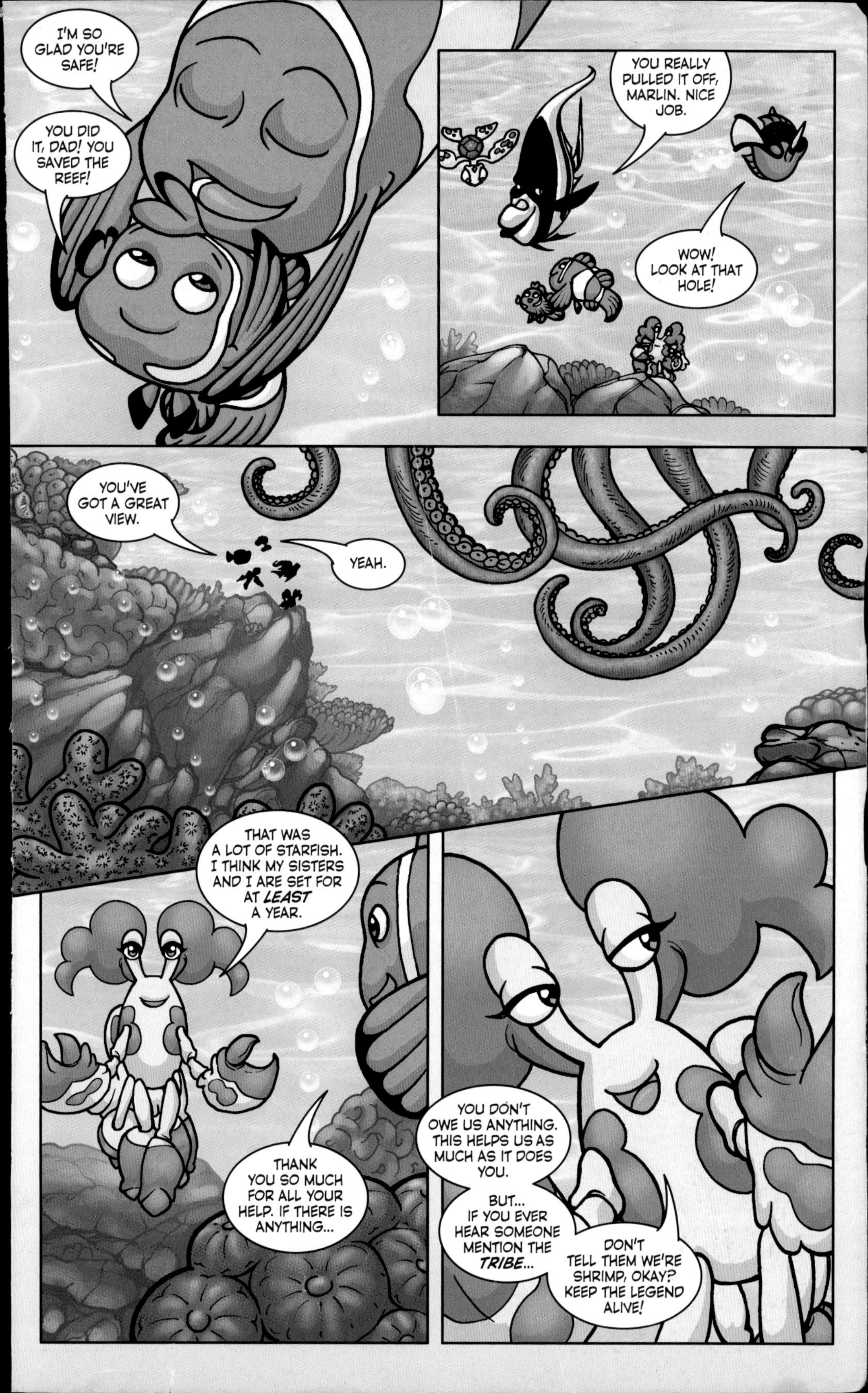
I'M SO GLAD YOU'RE SAFE!
YOU DID IT, DAD! YOU SAVED THE REEF!
YOU REALLY PULLED IT OFF, MARLIN. NICE JOB.
WOW! LOOK AT THAT HOLE!
YOU'VE GOT A GREAT VIEW.
YEAH.
THAT WAS A LOT OF STARFISH. I THINK MY SISTERS AND I ARE SET FOR AT *LEAST* A YEAR.
THANK YOU SO MUCH FOR ALL YOUR HELP. IF THERE IS ANYTHING...
YOU DON'T OWE US ANYTHING. THIS HELPS US AS MUCH AS IT DOES YOU.
BUT... IF YOU EVER HEAR SOMEONE MENTION THE *TRIBE*...
DON'T TELL THEM WE'RE SHRIMP, OKAY? KEEP THE LEGEND ALIVE!

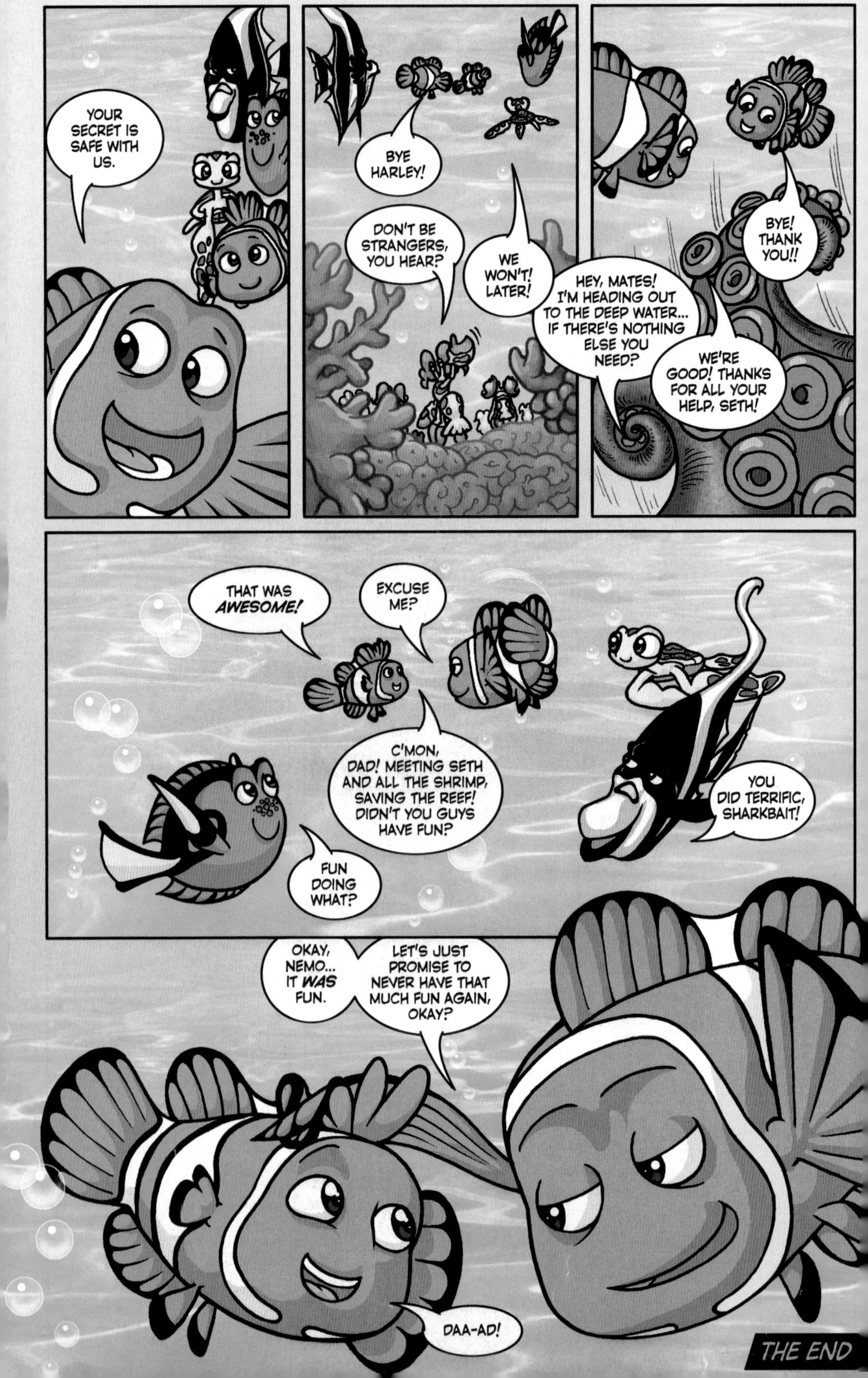
YOUR SECRET IS SAFE WITH US.
BYE HARLEY!
DON'T BE STRANGERS, YOU HEAR?
WE WON'T! LATER!
HEY, MATES! I'M HEADING OUT TO THE DEEP WATER... IF THERE'S NOTHING ELSE YOU NEED?
BYE! THANK YOU!!
WE'RE GOOD! THANKS FOR ALL YOUR HELP, SETH!
THAT WAS *AWESOME!*
EXCUSE ME?
C'MON, DAD! MEETING SETH AND ALL THE SHRIMP, SAVING THE REEF! DIDN'T YOU GUYS HAVE FUN?
FUN DOING WHAT?
YOU DID TERRIFIC, SHARKBAIT!
OKAY, NEMO... IT *WAS* FUN.
LET'S JUST PROMISE TO NEVER HAVE THAT MUCH FUN AGAIN, OKAY?
DAA-AD!
THE END

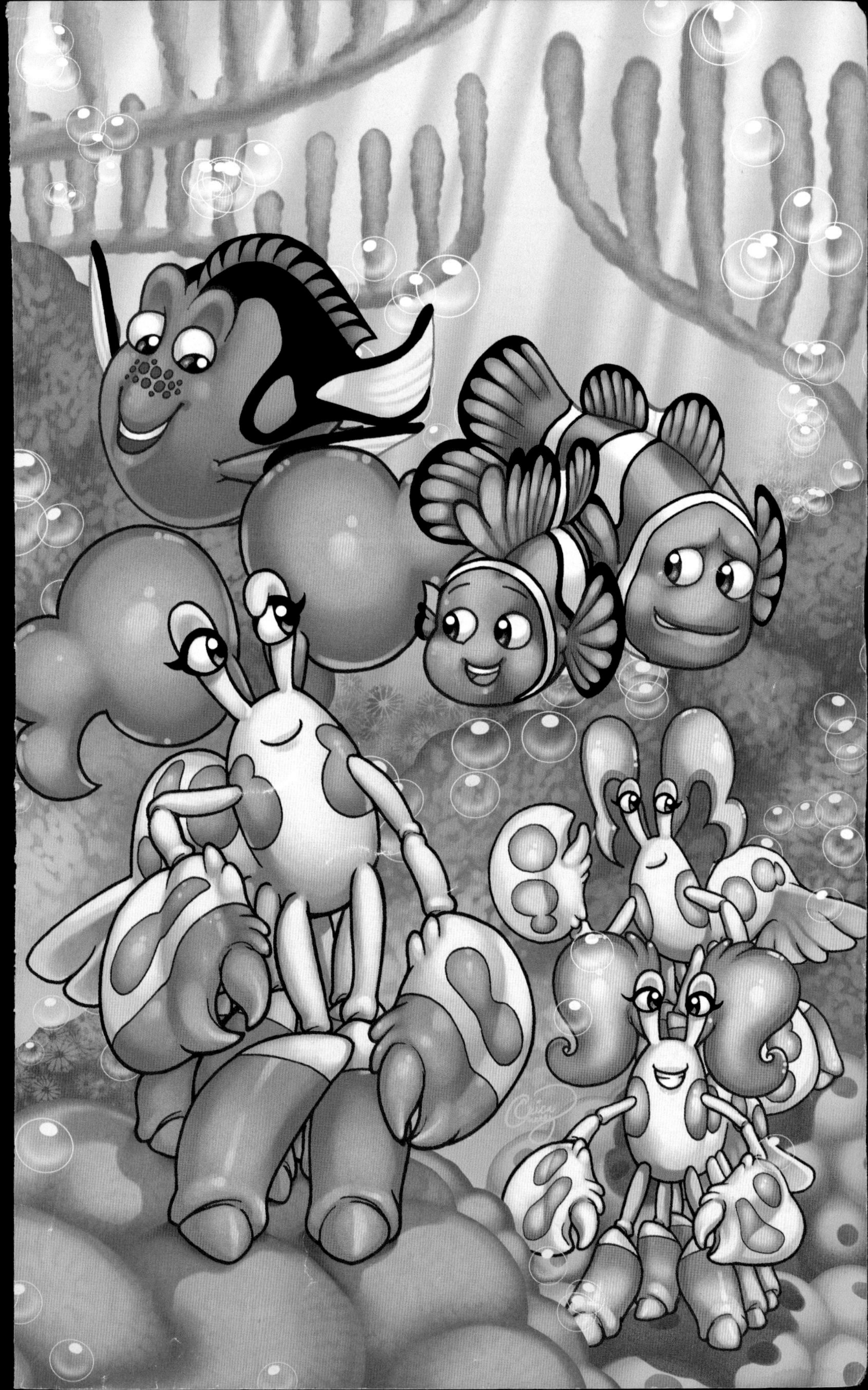

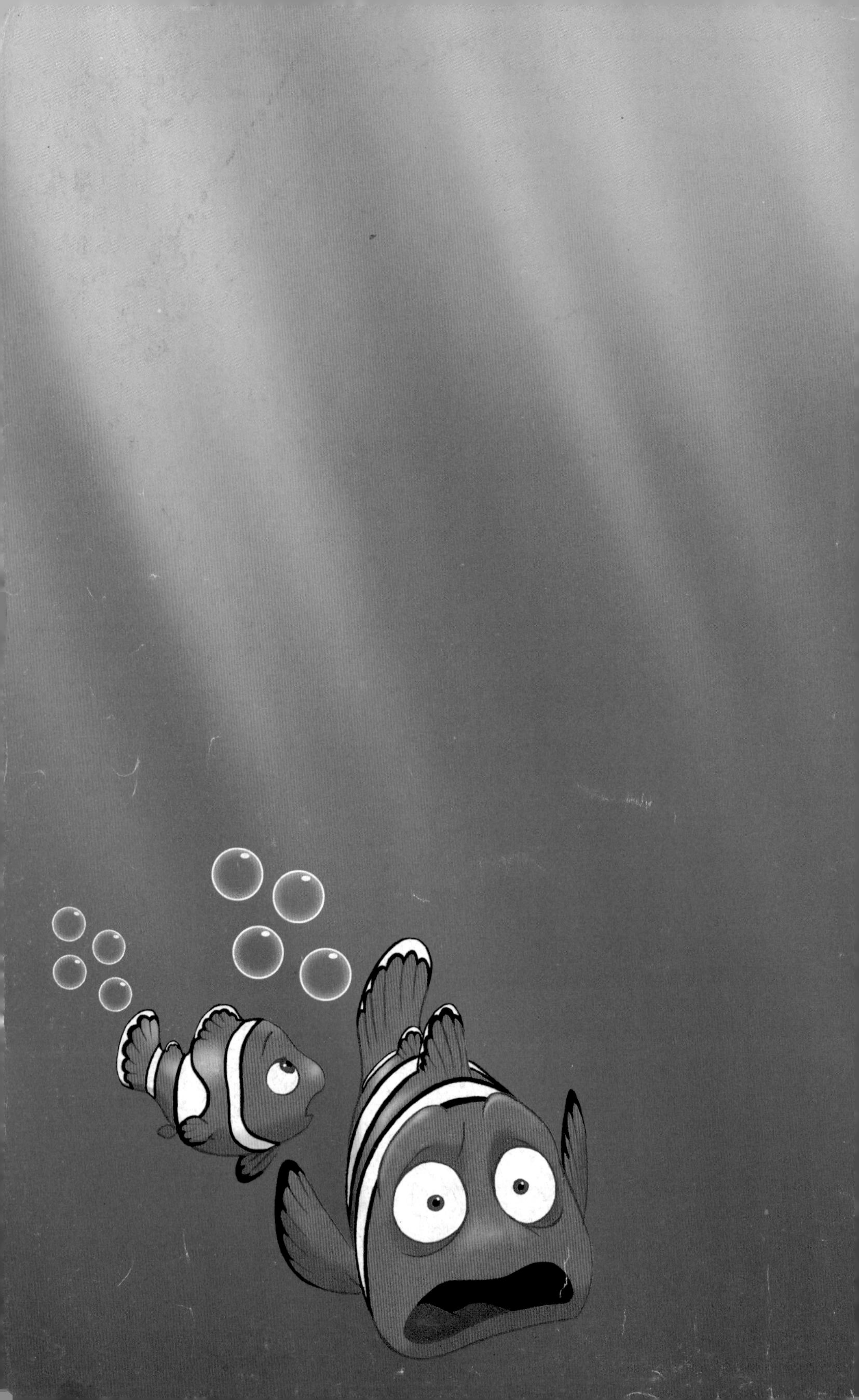

Disney · PIXAR

# FINDING NEMO

## REEF RESCUE

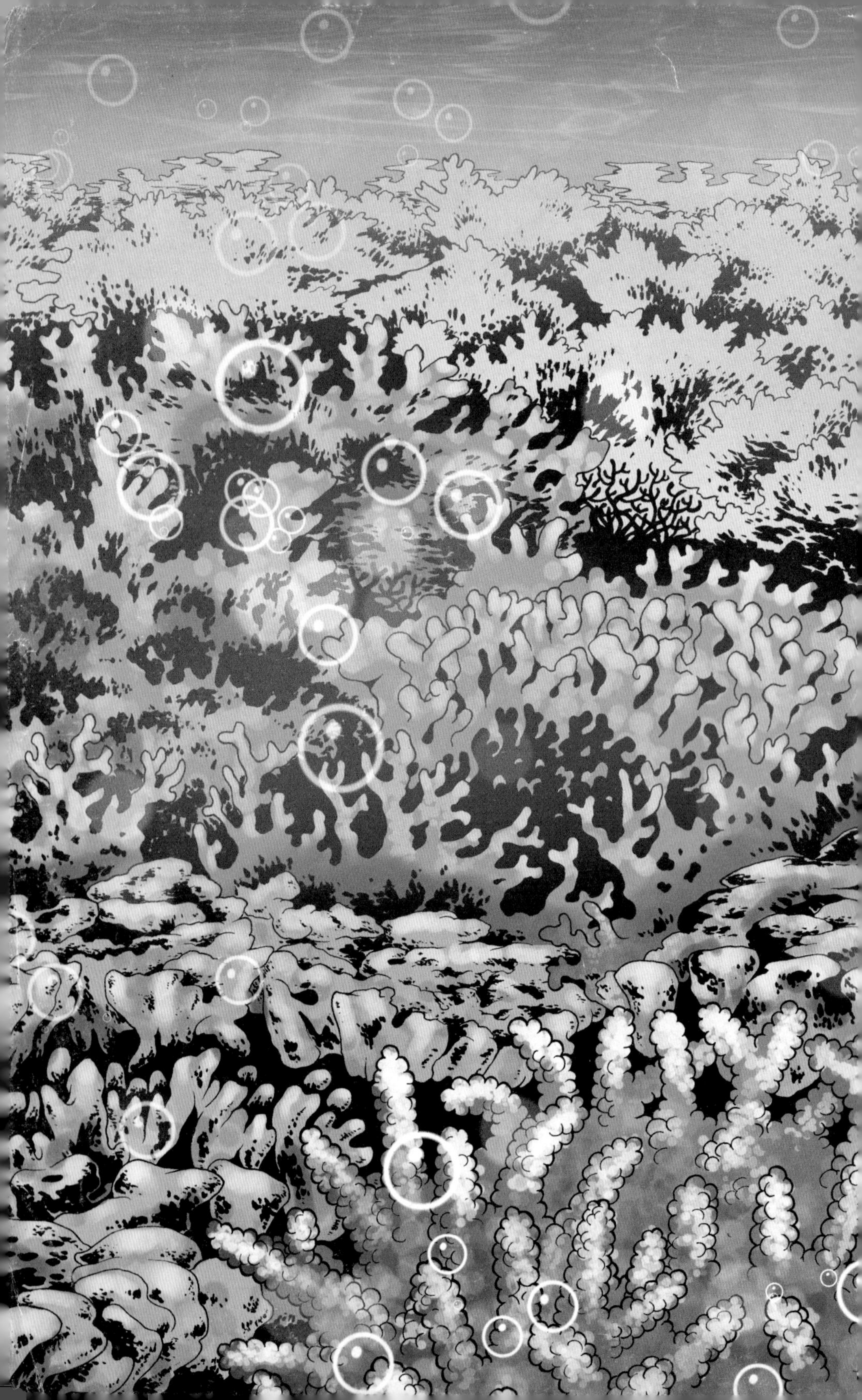